MW00884851

Becoming Kimberly

A TRANSGENDER'S JOURNEY

Kimberly Davis

ISBN: 1546894691

ISBN 13: 9781546894698

Preface

Before you read this narrative, there are some things you need to know. This is the story of both my life and my struggle to fit in as someone who was assigned male at birth but who was truly female in her heart. I learned to hide the parts that society rejected very early—from everyone but my parents. I never successfully hid things from them. I tried—oh brother, did I ever try.

This story takes me from my earliest childhood memory to the time as an adult when I was recovering from my version of gender-reassignment surgery. It will also explore what it was like to go back to work as a woman. Although the book covers a span of sixty-three years of my life, the actual transition process took about a full year, from June 2016 until June 2017.

The people mentioned in this book as coworkers are real people, and I used their real names. They all know me, so when they read the book (assuming they do), because they will know who I am talking about, I didn't bother changing their names. Their actions are as true as I can recollect. I highly respect my coworkers, some of the best professionals in healthcare. They are also damn fine people, both in and out of the hospital. I do sincerely hope none of them takes offense at anything I have said in this book, as most of it is from my viewpoint, and things change according to your viewpoint.

If I have unintentionally hurt anyone by something I wrote in this book, I do hereby, publicly and formally, issue a profound apology. I would ask those people to please remember that my book is about *my* transition from male to female. As such, it is written selfishly from my point of view.

This year has been a huge learning experience for me and for everyone I encountered from day to day. I have tried to be an educator, but sometimes I couldn't keep up. Questions seem to pop up faster than I can find answers.

As with any action, I understood going in that there would be a reaction. That's basic scientific law.

Since my transition, I have lost my sister. She has only spoken to me once since I came out, and that was to condemn me and tell me I was going to hell. I helped Mom raise that little girl, who was a baby when I was ten years old. I helped a lot. I tutored her in math in junior high. I taught her the multiplication tables. It was a shame that she got that far in school and did not know them already. I put her in the top 5 percent of her math class by the end of the school year, and she never had another problem with math. In fact, she now works in banking. I done good. But that is another story—and now that I am going to hell, none of that matters.

Most of my friends have stuck with me, and I have made plenty of new ones to make up for the losses. It still hurts to lose one. As one coworker recently put it:

> On your birthday, your coworkers gave you a crown with happy birthday on it. I had been wanting to have a conversation with you about your transition, and I had lots of questions but did not know how to start the conversation. When I saw you in the cafeteria that day with the crown, I just wished you a happy birthday and the conversation took off. You were so warm and open. Without embarrassment, you answered all my questions. I quickly realized that the same warm, tender, loving heart that beat in Richard was also beating in Kimberly and I knew you were all right.

(Sorry, Pat, but even though I paraphrased that a bit, what you wrote was so sweet, it made me cry from joy.)

Please enjoy this book. I hope it gives you some insight into my world and the transgender world in general. We have come a long way, but we have a long way to go, still. Don't hesitate to drop me an e-mail. I will answer if I can. (Please keep them short and to the point.) You can reach me via author services at Amazon.com.

If you like this book, please encourage someone else to buy a copy. I do have cat food to buy, and there are always taxes to pay. After all, someone must.

With all my love,
Kimberly Davis
Brinson, Georgia
June 2017

This book is dedicated to the love of my life, Victoria Virginia Genge-Davis. I would not be here if you had not lovingly brought me twenty-five years down the road.
It is also dedicated to all the members of the LGBTQ community who have lost their lives to ignorance, violence, and depression so that we may all be out in the open and walk forward to the future with our heads held high (and for some of us, our tits out too).

Long live the rainbow.
—KD

Chapter One

Who Am I?

Who am I?

This question only came to the forefront of my life just two short months ago. On June 1, 2016, my loving wife of nearly twenty-five years departed this life after a very brief battle with breast cancer. Suddenly, I found myself alone with the only person I knew extremely well (or so I thought). What did not become immediately apparent was that I was about to face the greatest loss of identity I have ever experienced.

Without warning, I realized that I had no identity. I did not know who I was or what I wanted to do with the rest of my life. Since birth, I have lived at someone else's beck and call. For the first twenty years of my life, I answered to my parents. I lived in their home and mostly danced to their tune. My time with them was, of course, very necessary, and I would not be where I am today without them and their love for me. Looking back, they did not have an easy time with me, but I'll have more about that later.

When I was about twenty-two, I started dating a girl who was a bit more experienced in life than I, even though I was older. Boy, did I learn things from her. The sex was wonderful. *I want it, I need it,* I thought, *so let's get married so's I can have sex all the time.* She was sixteen and still under her father's watchful eye, so things were a bit tricky, but we managed to find alone time. A year and a few months later, we were married and started a rocky journey through life. The years went by, and the children came along—three of them, to be exact. I worked hard to make a living for the family, but I was severely handicapped by circumstances beyond my control. We scratched out a survival existence, but we did survive.

Five years down that road, the lawyers got involved. We got a divorce (after I bought her a house, of course). Well, she got the house, the car and the kids. Me? I got the child support and very few choices. I had no place to live at this point but my car, so I ended up back at my mom's. She took me in and gave me a bed to sleep in and food to eat. You gotta love moms. They are great, aren't they? Always there when you need them—until they aren't. So now I was single and broke. I was working eighteen hours a day but still broke. I needed to find someone to live with, but as they say, "You can't fish without bait," and I was flat busted. (I hope I made the point that I was penniless; I certainly tried.)

I somehow managed to start a successful construction company with my brother. A couple of years in, we had money. As soon as my ex-wife found out I had money (and she wasn't able to get any of it), she dumped the kids on me to raise and hauled ass out of state with her boyfriend. After that, I had a business to run and three young boys to raise.

A couple of years later, as I was searching for some adult company, I found the love of my life. That discovery and relationship is a subject for another book, so I will not go into details here. Just know that this lady was what I had always needed in my life.

The first few years of any relationship are always up and down (that's what keeps divorce attorneys in business). Vikki and I wanted to hammer it out and live in harmony together, so we worked on it. We each brought baggage into the marriage. She had lost her daughter in a car accident the year before we got married, and I needed a woman's help in raising my three sons. She was never a great parent, but she gave it 110 percent. She gave all that she had to give. Undoubtedly, the hardest job on the planet is being a stepparent. I couldn't do it, I can tell you that. Suffice it to say, the childrearing put a terrific strain on our marriage.

A few years down the road, when the boys were grown, we moved to Daytona Beach to help care for her aging father. We went through it all together: her cancer and chemotherapy, her father's death, and an accident that basically left me jobless again. With Vikki's guidance and full support, I decided to go back to college and finish my degree, in hopes of gaining a better job and improving our lifestyle. I rented my cousin's house across from Mom, moved back to Georgia, and got back into school.

It's tough for someone who's forty-eight to go to school with young 'uns, but I did. As one of my friends put it, it was "five years of living on air." Thanks to the student-loan program and part-time work, we made it work and lived reasonably comfortably. With college finished and a job as a nuclear medicine technologist at a regional hospital that provided a comfortable income, Vikki and I suddenly had resources that made a huge difference in our lives. We had fun together and could afford to do some of the things we always wanted to do. We acquired a house and property, and all we owed each year was property taxes (and they were not very high). With our vehicles all paid off, we had extra discretionary income, and we used it on occasion.

Life was good. No, life was *grand*. The grandkids came along, and we enjoyed them, although we rarely got to see them. Just when things started to look rosy, the shit hit the fan. My life is no exception. In 2014, Vikki was diagnosed with lupus. Sometime after the beginning of 2016, she started failing. Because we assumed it was the lupus flaring up, we treated it accordingly with increasing amounts of pain meds. By mid-March, I knew we were in trouble. I kept insisting that we take her to the emergency room and find out what was wrong, but she kept putting me off. Finally, on April 6, she agreed to go the next day.

April 7, 2016, brought devastation into my life.

At the emergency room of the hospital where I work, the ER doctor examined her and ordered a CT scan of her abdomen. I went with her to the CT room. A good friend of mine was running the scanner, so I sat in the control room and watched as the scanner produced images that would forever devastate my life. Several soft-tissue masses were displayed, as well as a couple of bone lesions.

It was cancer.

A few days later, we were told it was stage-4 breast cancer. Although her oncologist was optimistic, the lesions were everywhere. We counted thirteen different lesions on her PET scan. This stuff was aggressive—and how. We tried chemo for three weeks, and each week, Vikki got weaker and weaker. Finally, in the fourth week, as we drove to the oncology office for bloodwork, Vikki told me that she did not want to continue the treatments. She said she was weary and bone tired. She just wanted to go home, go to bed, go to sleep—and not wake up. I told her that the decision had to be hers and that whatever she decided, I would support her. Her doctor talked her into calling in hospice, and we did. Hospice came and evaluated her the next day and set up the orders for pain control. They were wonderful. For the rest of Vikki's life, we kept her pain free and comfortable. She passed away two weeks later, quietly and in her sleep.

This event is what precipitated my quandary. For the first time in my life, I was truly alone and without direction. I took no orders from anyone, and I did not have to take requests from anyone. *So how do I find out who I am? Where should I look to find the person I have suddenly become?* The answers to these and many other questions would be difficult to find. I am still searching for some of them. I began my quest by looking back to the beginning, and that is where I will take you. Buckle up, cupcake: it gets rocky from here on in.

I was born in 1953, the oldest of three siblings. My father was a Korean War vet (although he never served outside the United States). He was drafted and basically spent his entire active duty going to one school or another. He married my mother while he was in the army. Two or three years later, they had me. Dad built a house on some land given to him by his mom and basically paid for the house as he went along, scrounging material where he could. It took a couple of years, and when we moved in, only one bedroom was finished. By then, I had a baby brother. My brother and I slept in the bedroom, while Mom and Dad bunked down in the living room. Two or three years later, Dad finished the master bedroom.

At birth, I was named Richard Kimberly Davis. My parents called me Kim, and that is the name I went by until years later, when I went back to college at age forty-eight. Even Vikki called me Kim. Although I asked my mom why they hung a feminine name on me, I never got a straight answer. When I started back to college, I started going by Richard. Everyone at the hospital where I work knew me by that name. Talk about a split personality—I have one. I was Richard at work and Kim everywhere else. Whoa! (At least I didn't get the nickname "Dick.") I introduced myself to a girl once and said, "Hi, I am Richard, or Dick for short."

She said, "How do you get Dick out of Richard?"

I replied, "Try dinner and a movie. That will work for sure."

From my earliest memory, I have had a peculiar liking for girls' clothes. Mom used to find her undies in the strangest of places. At first, it was only underwear, because they were so readily available. This "problem" went on through puberty, young adulthood, and my early college years. My parents thought I was gay. Little did they know—and they didn't bother to find out. I am sure they talked to their doctors about me. Although I don't know for sure, I am pretty sure they got some particularly bad advice. What they chose to do was sweep it under the rug and not talk to me about my "problem." They hoped and prayed it would just go away.

When I started dating and having sex with a woman, my dad had to have been relieved that his oldest son was not a homosexual. He even went to my young bride shortly after we were married and thanked her for "making a man" out of me. (That scared the hell out of her, let me tell you!) She later found out what it was all about. She couldn't handle it any better than my parents could, so eventually, she divorced me.

During the marriage, I found out that I liked wearing women's clothes—not just underwear, but dresses and slacks and heels. They felt so nice. It was not about the sex; it was about how I felt while wearing them. I felt comfortable. It was a real Zen moment. The problem was the social stigma that accompanied this.

After I married Vikki, she and I had a conversation about the clothes thing. Although she was a liberal old hippie who tried to understand, she couldn't be comfortable with it. Because I truly loved her, I eventually suppressed the urges. I disposed of my underwear collection. (That sounds creepy, doesn't it?) At this point, I still was not collecting ladies' wear, just underwear. I used to get some strange looks when shopping in the ladies' sections at Walmart or Goodwill. Society still had not made the adjustment. Even though the law now supports transgender individuals, most of society still looks at us like we are lepers.

I recently heard comments about the new bathroom laws allowing transgender people to use the restroom of the gender they identify as: transgender people should be allowed to use the restroom of the sex they identify as, instead of the one listed on their birth certificate. One redneck said, "No pervert is gonna go in the bathroom with my daughter. I won't stand for him in there ogling her." Sorry, bud, but that transgender person is not interested in ogling your little girl. She just wants to pee, fix her makeup, and brush her hair. I will guarantee that your little girl is safer in there with a trans woman than with your redneck brother or nephew, because for sure and for certain, she is not interested in having sex with a kid. I am not so sure about your brother or nephew—and that is a cold, hard, provable fact.

(Sorry, I got sidetracked. It happens.)

After Vikki died, I had to clean out our house. There were so many things to do. My oldest son and oldest grandson helped me put all Vikki's clothes in plastic bags and load them onto the truck to haul to Goodwill. Now I wish I had been a bit more selective with what I threw away. I thought I had all her clothes out of the house, but later on, I found more and more, including a couple of bras and a swimsuit or two.

When I realized what I had found, and after thinking about it for a bit, I went shopping. I stopped by the Salvation Army and bought some bras and some skirts. I went to Goodwill and bought a couple of dresses (some of which actually almost fit). Talk about clueless; I was *clueless*. I had no idea what size I wore. I had no idea what size to buy. I bought a bunch of stuff that simply was too small and I couldn't wear. And then there are shoes. Do you know that a man's shoe size and a woman's shoe size are different? I do now. God, did my feet hurt! I'm still trying to get a handle on that. Even if I bought the right size, they did not always fit my feet, because different styles of ladies' shoes fit differently.

The learning curve on this is so steep as to be unbelievable, but I am learning. How my life changed when I found that I could order stuff from Amazon and HSN and have it delivered to my house! No longer did I have to endure the looks from the salesladies who looked at me like I was a pervert who was pawing through the underwear racks. *This is cool,* I thought. *I can order false boobs made from silicone that feel and weigh like the real things—almost.* With the right bra and blouse, I defy you to tell me they are not real. They even jiggle right. You can get stick-on adhesive so you can go braless, but I have not found that to work very well.

This guy is sick! I can hear some of you thinking. *He wants to dress up like a woman and go pick up men somewhere.* (Well, that's what women do, right?) Sorry to disappoint you; being transgender is not about *sex.* Never has been and never will be. Sure, there is sex involved, but let's be honest here: sex is in most everything, from cigarettes to pantyhose. In fact, sex was invented to sell stockings. Some of us male-to-female (MTF) transgenders still like women. On the other hand, some of us want to pick up men and have sex with them. Some of us go either way (and they represent the "B" in LGBT).

I am a transgender person who likes women. The question then becomes if I take this transition through gender reassignment surgery, would that make me a lesbian? At my age, I am probably not going to do gender reassignment surgery (GRS for short). At some point, after I retire, I will get a facelift. I'll have my nose done and get a boob job. Those falsies are a royal pain in the ass. If I can't re-sculpt my waist with diet and exercise, I may have that fixed as well. There is a lot of shit possible with plastic surgery these days. Oh, by the way, one of the famous "Bond girls" is a MTF transgender person, but I won't tell you which one. You have to figure it out—and trust me, you will never guess just by looking at her.

One of my coworkers is openly lesbian. One of our doctors is openly gay. Maybe more than one, I do not know and am too polite to ask. Your personal life is none of my business. The things I am writing about are just some of the things that may help you ask yourself some serious questions about who you are. This narrative is the story of my journey. At this point, I had just begun to take the first baby steps in a years-long trip that would cover monumental distances. I am moving from the man I used to be to the woman I wish to become. It will only be a partial journey for me, sadly, because I can't do some of the things I would have done had I started on this trip many years ago. Maybe I didn't have the courage. I certainly didn't have the money (and trust me, it takes a bunch). Maybe I had to wait for the time to be right.

All I know for sure is that I have spent far too much time being Richard. It is now time to become Kimberly. Please join me on this journey. It will not always be pleasant or pretty, but I promise you, it will always be real.

Chapter Two

Beginning Adventures

I got dressed up a few weeks ago and started looking around for the accessories every woman must have: purses, wallets, watches, rings, necklaces, earrings, and the like. The first thing I found was a shoebox full of some of Vikki's costume jewelry. My Vikki did have some nice stuff at one time in her life, when it was important to her, but now it's a bit dated. As dated as it was, it still worked for learning about fashion. Fashion is going to be fun to learn, but it is going to take a great deal of time and energy, as there is a lot to learn. I have always been a blue jeans and T-shirt kind of guy (at least, Richard was). Kimberly, however, is starting to look like she'll be quite the clothes horse!

I have a female friend who really goes wild with shoes and handbags. She loves the expensive ones. All of them. I can't wait to tell her that I truly understand how she feels. Well, maybe I can. Finding a friend you can trust with a secret this big is tricky. You never know how supposedly intelligent, educated people will react, and I am not sure she can handle this. I still have to work for several more years before retirement. I can't afford to lose my job, so I have to be very, very careful about who learns my secret.

One night a couple of weeks ago, I got all gussied up, put on my favorite black pants (the ones with the stripes), a black maternity top (because it fits my current upper body better and is less revealing), a nice pair of shoes (that *almost* fit), and I went out on the town. Not the town I live in or work in, but one in another state that's sixty miles from the house. Nobody knows me in this other town. I could go anywhere I wanted, so I went to dinner at the Chinese restaurant that used to be our favorite, and then I went shopping at Target. I have been a loyal Target shopper for years. They have about the same prices as Walmart, but the merchandise is much better, and the people shopping there dress better. I do not know if I successfully "passed" as a woman, but nobody commented one way or the other. I am still learning how to walk like a woman, and there is a lot to that. I am a long way from sounding like one.

The evening out took a great deal of courage. I would say "it took balls," but I am trying to ignore that part of me right now. The last thing I want to hear is, "Hey, lady, your balls are hanging out of your drawers. You might want to do something about that."

On several occasions, the people I interacted with treated me like a lady. This was encouraging, as I tried not to say much. I'm still trying to sound like a female. The good news is I have a naturally high tenor voice, but it has deepened in the last few years. So now I must reverse that trend and try to learn to pitch my voice higher. This will not be easy, but I need to just do it until I can do it without thinking about it. My voice must become as instinctive as my walk must be.

That walk—oh my God! Women move their arms much more than men do, and they walk much more rhythmically. That bedonkadonk must *swing*—not *too* much, mind you, but just enough to be alluring. The walk should be good enough to fool anyone, even another woman. Trust me, it's easy enough to do when you are thinking about it, but it is extremely hard to learn to do this instinctively. It takes massive amounts of repetition.

Richard has a personality. He is a good and funny man. A natural-born comedian, he almost missed his calling to do standup comedy. He would have been successful at it, I promise. Richard is a gentleman and does the gentlemanly things instinctively. He opens doors, pulls out the chairs, picks up the dropped handkerchief, and does these things without thinking about them.

Kimberly is a virgin in every definition of the word. She knows absolutely nothing about being sexy, alluring, and all the other things that go into being a woman. All these things she must learn, most of them the hard way. Truth be told, I do not want to entice a man into having sex with me. That is absolutely the last thing I want. I just want to be accepted as a serious, sexy woman who is fun to be around. I want my personality to tell people that this woman is someone you *need* to know.

I haven't a clue how to go about creating this person. At this point, I am seeking professional help. Somewhere out there is a psychologist who can help me evolve a personality for Kimberly. (As I write this, I am looking forward to meeting with one next Wednesday.) She is planning to help Richard deal with his grief and the loss of his wife, but maybe she can help Kimberly with her little problem as well.

I wanted to get my ears pierced so I could wear some jewelry there. I tried to do this myself. I had a bottle of lidocaine, so I didn't think there would be a problem. I succeeded in puncturing my earlobes without too much pain and was able to get the earrings in, but then I ran into a problem: you have to wear them for three to six weeks for the holes to heal and become permanent, and I didn't have the right studs to insert. After all the agony, I asked a friend where to go, and she gave me some good advice. Now I have diamond studs in both ears. After all, diamonds are a girl's second-best friend. Thank you, my good friend, for the advice.

Back to this personality thing. I don't have a clue how to proceed. I do not want to let it evolve naturally, because I do not yet have the freedom to do so. I have to continue to be Richard at work. I also have to be Richard during most of my life; I just can't deal with the consequences of becoming Kimberly in the open at this point. I am afraid. The repercussions at work would be embarrassing, and I am not sure I could survive it. I do not need that kind of pressure, and I'm not sure it would be healthy. So, for the next five years, I have to lead a double life. I have to be careful. That road leads to insanity, and I do not want to walk down that path. Although maybe I already am insane. I have considered this point. Maybe I am bat-shit crazy. Maybe I need to be locked up.

That is the way most conservatives see me. "You are fucking nuts, you pervert, you. You need to be shot, hung, and locked up for the rest of your life." Sorry, folks, but that is not true at all. I am not insane, have never been insane, and will not go insane. I am not gay. I am not a pedophile. I will not molest your sons and daughters. This brings us to the next topic. While I am on my soapbox, I wish to speak to all you right-wing conservatives.

I am one of you.

In most respects, I am conservative. I vote Republican most of the time. Sometimes, when there is a Democratic candidate who deserves the office, I vote for them. I am pro-choice. I do not believe the government has the right to tell a woman what she can do with her body. If it were a man, there would be no question at all, right? Why is there a question with women? I would not want to have a baby if I deemed it untimely or distasteful. Why should I? (This is ignoring the fact that due to biology, having a baby would be impossible for me.) I still want to be a woman, even with the down side. This I will do, come hell or high water.

I told my best friend that I was writing a book, and she promised to read it when I am done. This process is very therapeutic, I think. It's already helped me get my thoughts organized. I have a grief-counseling session soon, and I have debated whether or not I should show up in drag and say, "Yes, we need to discuss my grief, but we have another problem that needs addressing as well." I still have not decided to or not to do this. I will let you know later how it turns out.

I have not started hormone-replacement therapy (HRT) at this point, but I am taking over-the-counter remedies. We will see how that works out. I have to find a testosterone blocker, because I am not yet willing to part with the boys. I think that will come at some point, but that will be down the road a bit. I have a cruise booked for spring 2017, and I have already asked a woman to accompany me. I do expect this will involve sex and am looking forward to this encounter. Like I said earlier, I am transgender, not gay. I still love women and very much enjoy looking at a good-looking female. I will never get over that. I am wired that way. I do not ever want to have sex with a man, and I'm still trying to figure that out.

Trying to separate Richard from Kimberly is difficult at this point. Somewhere down the road, a few years from now, Richard will cease to be, and Kimberly will be the dominant personality, but that is way off. I still have to figure out just who Kimberly is. At this point, I need professional help (not the psychiatric kind, but the psychological kind). For those who do not know the difference, a psychiatrist helps people with their mental illness. A psychologist helps people modify their behavior to make it acceptable to society. Thank goodness transgenderism is becoming accepted by the mainstream.

Finally, we are not perverts and sexual deviants. My God, but this has been hard on us. Please accept us for who we are. We are good people, and most of us simply want to be left alone to live our lives and associate with people of like temperament and mind. We don't wish to be vilified for what we wear or who we pretend to be. That is the point: we are not "pretending." This is who we are. All you have to do is be tolerant and accept us. Don't judge us; you have no right. We don't judge you, no matter how prejudiced you are. See how easy it is to judge people? If you are reading this text, you have already proved that you have an open mind. You have proved that you are not prejudiced. It is so easy to judge people who are not following your chosen path. Robert Frost said in one of his poems, "Two roads diverged in a wood, and I—I took the one less traveled by." That is what I did, only it took me years and years to get here.

I got sidetracked on being me because of the love of a wonderful person. She was female and gloriously so. Vikki enjoyed sex, anytime, anyplace, and any way. She was damn good at it too. She kept me happily satisfied for twenty-five years. Sex with her was a bunch of things, but it was never boring. I have heard men say they were bored by their sex lives, but I wasn't—ever. In many ways, we had a "same-sex marriage," because we always had the "the same sex." But I was never bored. We enjoyed every intimate moment together and we were very good together. Even after we got old and fat and out of shape, we found ways to accommodate each other. One of the highlights of our life together was that she was finally successful in giving me a blow job to completion. Vikki had Temporomandibular Joint Disorder commonly referred to as TMJ which complicated that part of our sex life. I had a few hang-ups about it. When she managed to actually pull it off (or suck it off, so to speak), she was very happy. (So was I, come to think of it.) It was very nice.

I am not particularly looking for sex at this point, although it would not be unwelcome. I am trying to figure out who I am and what I want. Sex is not very high on the list right now. Other things are much more pressing. I have to learn so many things, all of them new and very few of them things I learned as a child. Given the fact that I was raised as a male (well, I had male plumbing, didn't I?), I missed out on all the girl lessons about brushing hair, hair care in general, skincare, periods (I will not miss that), fitting clothing, underwear, what goes where, makeup, how to walk and talk and gesture, facial expressions, and just about everything else. What little I know, I learned from watching other girls and living with two of the species. I have been sitting down to pee for years now, so that comes naturally. When I started doing that, it just felt more natural than standing up. Another sign of my gender misalignment, I guess.

Kimberly must develop naturally, but she will need some help along the way. I already have the help and advice of one very good friend, someone I trust completely. Someday soon, I promise, she will get to meet Kimberly. She already knows Richard very well, and I can't wait for her to meet Kimberly. Kimberly will also need professional help and advice, and I hope I make the first step down that path on Wednesday. I trust that the person I meet with will be an open-minded professional who will give me some good advice and direction. I have a lifetime to make up and not much time left to get the job done. Now, see that is a man talking. A woman would not worry about getting the work done; she would want to look damn good doing it.

It's the little things, isn't it? It's always the little things that trip us up. Little things like a penis and testicles can get in the way of living life to the fullest. If men are from Mars, and women are from Venus, where do transgenders come from? The moon!

After all, according to the religious right, we are "looney" and need to be locked up (if not burned at the stake). Yes, they would, and I can prove it. They burned Joan of Arc as a heretic for wearing men's armor into battle—a battle she won, by the way. The Baptist minister down the road, with whom I grew up, would light the damn fire himself—and he's a "good guy." I am not picking on the Baptists; most of the Christian religions would happily stack the wood. And Muslims? Forget it; they are worse. Per Wikipedia, the Quran regards homosexuality as a sin but does not spell out any punishment. Muslim countries run the gamut from the death penalty to stoning to being thrown from high places. Some Muslim countries have laws protecting the rights of homosexuals, lesbians, and transgender persons. Although many of the Muslim countries have the death penalty on the books, the laws are seldom enforced. All the Quran said about transgender men and women was to "turn them out of your house". Most of the laws are based not on the Quran, but on the human interpretation of the writings.

I turned gray early. My hair started graying in my midtwenties and never stopped. By the time Vikki and I got married, it was nicely salt and pepper, but that didn't last long. By fifty, it was solid white. I kept it short while in school and in the early years of my career, but a few years ago, I decided to let it grow. I wanted a mullet like MacGyver; that man had a nice head of hair.

Once it started to grow, I lost interest in the mullet style and just let it grow. Vikki loved it and enjoyed playing with my curls. My hair is thick and has great natural curls and body. I will never have to have a perm. At work, I pull it back into a ponytail, but as soon as I am in the car on the way home, the scrunchie comes off, and the brush comes out of my purse. Freed, my hair looks great. Yes, I carry a purse. How else am I going to carry my lipstick, makeup, compact mirror, wipes, extra jewelry for emergencies, cell phone, keys, and so on? I used to fuss at Vikki about all the junk in her purse and how much it weighed. I have one myself now and need a larger one to carry all the shit I have packed in the damn thing.

Anyway, back to the hair. I have a great stylist. He is a good friend and takes good care of my hair, but he is still thinking in terms of male styles. I may have to find another stylist to get the female style I want, but that will come much later. Robbie is good for now, but he would not understand just who I am becoming.

So, for now, my hair will continue to be long, white, and flowing when I am off work. My nails, on the other hand, are going to be a problem. I play the guitar, and that requires that I keep them short. I also can't paint them. My toenails are in bad shape, and I must work on them, especially if I want to wear some of the toeless shoes that look so good. I will be very glad when I can do a mani-pedi. Just like everything else about this transitional period, it is going to take a lot of time.

One of the first things that Kimberly will need, besides clothes and shoes, will be a voice. Before she can have a personality, she must be able to speak eloquently and sound like a lady, because she most definitely is a lady, whatever else she may be. The voice will take a great deal of practice, and I do not even know where to begin. The good news is that there are actually resources out on the Internet that will help her learn how to speak. The rest of the personality development, I do not know about.

I do not have time to let Kimberly develop a personality the old-fashioned way, I have to force feed it and nurture it along to make sure it comes out right. All of this must be done in the shortest possible time. I probably need professional help. Because of my work situation, I may have to maintain Richard's personality over the next few years as I am developing Kimberly's new one. I think I can gradually start downplaying Richard's personality as time goes by and picking up some of Kimberly's mannerisms, without giving too much away. Retirement never seemed so far away as it does right now, but I know it will be here long before I am ready unless I get a move on. There is so much to do.

Tomorrow is the first grief-counseling session; this should prove interesting. I did find that there is indeed a provider in my area who works with transgender persons such as myself. However, I chose another provider.

I have so many problems to deal with, and I am not sure if my kids will understand. I know one of them will have a problem with this, but the other two might be okay. Sadly, the one who lives closest to me is the one who will have the issues with calling me Mom. I truly will not ask them to do that. I have been their dad for all of their lives, and it has been rewarding. I do not want to mother them now; I think I already did too much of that as they were growing up. I will miss going fishing with my son, though. We did have a lot of fun, and he loves it very much. He will still go with his lady and family, but I can't tag along.

This started out to be a daily journal about my transition. I think it has turned into a book. It's becoming a story of the incredibly difficult choices, the insane amount of hard work, and some of the wrong turns I will make traveling down this path. This is to be the story of my journey from one life into another. Maybe reading about my pitfalls will help you avoid the same ones. Of course, feel free to make all new mistakes. I am sure that you will. (Somehow, I lost sight of the book and just started rambling. Chapter 1 went well, but it has been downhill from there.)

A footnote to this chapter: when shaving your pits with an electric razor's sideburn trimmer, be very careful: the razor burn will scar you for life. Also, do not splash 90 percent rubbing alcohol on the freshly shaved pit. A blue streak of cussing does not help, but is involuntary. The burning sensation subsides after a couple of hours.

Another footnote: Put on some sweet perfume and a gold bracelet or two, and relax and enjoy yourself. You took another step today. Progress, always progress.

Chapter Three

Buh-Bye, Richard

Before I can fully embrace Kimberly, I must say good-bye to Richard. This is not as easy as you might think. Richard has been around for a long time, and overall, he is a good guy. In fact, as guys go, he is one in a million. Vikki thought so, and I valued her opinion over just about anyone I know. Richard has a big heart, as big as Texas. He will give you the shirt off his back, and if necessary, the pants off his bottom. In fact, his generosity is one of his biggest problems, as it interferes with the accumulation of material wealth. Vikki used to fuss at Richard for giving the children too much financial help. She wanted to help too, but she was more concerned about our financial stability.

Oftentimes, she was more right than Richard was. Let us try to understand Richard a bit better by going back to the beginning. This will also help you to understand Kimberly better.

"Step right into the WABAC machine, Sherman."

"Thank you, Mr. Peabody."

With that, here we go—all the way back to 1953.

When I was born, I was named Richard Kimberly Davis. I ate regularly, crapped a lot, and grew, oh so slowly, older year by year. I do not remember what year I discovered that I liked Mom's underwear. They were so nice and silky soft, but I do remember her catching me with them in bed and her reproving look as she took them away from me. As this occurred over and over again during my childhood, you'd think someone would have done something, but thank goodness, no one did. "Treatment" in those days was horrendously ineffective and involved shock therapy, bad drugs, and psychotherapy that was not worth ten cents and cost a hell of a lot more.

Dad was convinced I was gay. He spent a lot of sleepless nights, I am sure. I know he and Mom talked about my so-called perversion from time to time. Dad even talked to his doctor friends, and I am sure they fed him lots of extremely bad advice. During the time I was growing up, anybody who was not heterosexual was considered to be a pervert. In the 1960s, perversion was not to be tolerated in the Bible Belt South. Little boys didn't fool around with ladies' underwear. That was worse than incest. After all, if your sister ain't good enough for family, she ain't good enough for outsiders. (I am only being facetious, of course.) The point is that it was still very bad.

Puberty finally arrived, and with that came even more angst. All the raging hormones, pubic hair, and erections (especially those that occurred at the most embarrassing moments, like church, school, middle of the night—you know, when you least expect it). Oh, and wet dreams, or what they called "nocturnal emissions" in one text I read. Wet dreams were nice, very nice—but messy.

Puberty also brought a growing interest in the opposite sex, which was wonderful and heartbreaking all at the same time. Knowing that the girls were there and actually talking to one were two different things. At thirteen, the prospect of actually talking to a female human was one of the most frightening things I could have imagined. I simply would have died on the spot if one of them had up and kissed me.

Looking back, I wish I hadda knowed then what I know now. God, I would have been in so much trouble.

If Richard in junior high was bad enough, Richard in high school was so much worse. After two years in junior high, we got to go to the new high school. The building was nice and brand new. The girls were growing up and out, and so were some of the boys. PE was rough. I had to change into gym shorts in front of other guys and shower with them after sweating to the oldies or something like that. I was acutely aware of my nearly hairless body. For some unknown and unfair reason, my body hair was not growing very fast. It did eventually come in, and that helped, but mostly, it was after high school. I was what you would call a late bloomer. I was *very* late.

I met with some of my classmates a few months ago to plan our forty-fifth high school reunion this fall. Some of us wanted to do something this summer. We were in the middle of nailing down the plans when Vikki got diagnosed with cancer. I just about fell off the planet. Anyway, at one of our meetings, two of the girls and I were standing outside the restaurant, chatting. One of them happened to mention that they didn't remember me being this tall in high school. I wasn't. At the time, I was about five feet four inches tall (maybe five-five), and I weighed maybe 125 or 130 pounds.

I was definitely not going to be a high school football star, I was too short for basketball, and I couldn't see well enough for baseball. We didn't have a reading team, but I could have been captain. We didn't have a swim team when I was there, but the school did add one later. (My oldest son swam for them for four years. His letter jacket is hanging in my closet even now.) Given the chance, I would have been a swimming star. The one thing I could do physically was swim fast. I mean Mark Spitz fast. For those of you too young to remember Mark, he won five gold medals at the Olympics. Granted, this is nothing compared to Michael Phelps today, but Mark was a big deal in the early seventies. I once bought a stopwatch and timed myself. I beat Mark's medal times by a full second—and that is *fast*.

High school was filled with teenage angst, whatever the hell that means. I didn't particularly enjoy high school. Merely getting out of there with a diploma and grades good enough to get me into a college somewhere became my goal. The opposite sex had its own agenda, and I was not in on it. I kept thinking my time would come, but it never did. How did you go about learning this flirty, half-insulting kind of talk everyone (but me, it seemed) was doing?

There were no instructions with women: "Raise leg A to angle B and insert screw number two. When leg A is positioned firmly, raise leg B to the same angle on the other side and insert screw number two." With no owner's manual, I pretty much had to figure it out on the fly (so sorry about the bad pun). Instructions? They come with everything, it seems— but women and babies. I am sure women say the same thing about men. In fact, I have heard them make these comments.

Four years of relative hell went slowly by, and I finally graduated. I had been accepted to several colleges and looked forward to dorm life. With one or two notable exceptions, it was more high school, but it happened in different locations. I did, however, start to develop socially and made a few new friends, both male and female. I was still a virgin, though. I dated one girl for a brief time during the first spring semester. After she dropped out, we lost touch with each other over the summer. The underwear thing continued to rear its head, but I kept it private and was never caught at college. That would have been bad.

After a year of college, I dropped out and decided to go to technical school to learn electronics. I wanted to be chief engineer at a radio station or a television station. By this time, I was a professional DJ. I had my own radio show on weekends and soon got an afternoon show five days a week at a local country station. I did this for several years. The money was poor, and there was no glory at all. I was not good enough to syndicate or go to a big station, and I couldn't sell water in a desert.

Finally, I got out of the radio business and found a job working highway construction. I worked this for about a year. Once my brother graduated high school, Dad talked us into going into the construction business. Primarily, we did concrete finishing. Neither one of us knew how to finish concrete. I have actually had worse ideas. So, we both quit our jobs and bought a hundred dollars' worth of tools and started a concrete construction company. We actually built it into a successful business.

Three years into the business, I met a girl who would change my world forever. We ended up getting married, and after I sold out to my brother, we had three kids. It was never a happy marriage, but the sex was nice when it happened. Things happened during the marriage that forced me to learn about sex. Everything I have ever learned about people relations, I have had to do it the hard way. Most people learn to interact with the opposite sex almost instinctively. For me, it was a learned behavior, not an instinctive one. I didn't learn it the easy way; I had to dig for it.

Living with a woman gave me access to her underwear. I loved it. I also had access to her dresses, and I soon found out that I enjoyed that as well—until I got caught. At first, after she found my stash, she accused me of running around on her. In hindsight, I should have pleaded guilty and been more careful, but I told her the truth—and she couldn't handle it. This ultimately led to our divorce.

Skip ahead a few years, and I am living by myself in an apartment behind my mom's house. My ex-wife turns the boys over to me and leaves the state with her boyfriend. It takes a couple of weeks to finish setting up my mobile home in the woods, but we finish and move in. Living with the boys was great. I had my family back. Bunches of work for Dad, but loads of fun with my guys. Goodness gracious, I missed them terribly.

With the boys in the house, alone time was almost nonexistent. I ordered a few things from a J. C. Penney catalog and got on with my life. The boys provided a measure of peace to me, but as a red-blooded American male, I needed something more. I finally found a lady and we dated for a while. Well, mostly we just went to her house and had sex—which was great, mind you. At that point in my life, it was enough.

When Vikki came back into my life, I was actually dating someone else. I dropped Zelda like a hot potato. She and I had dated for several weeks and had yet to sleep together. She just kept putting me off for some reason. Although I didn't realize it at the time, the young lady had developed strong feelings for me and my boys. I did the one mean thing I ever did in my life.

Vikki and I were at her house, loading up her things to move in with me, when Zelda stopped by. She had seen my truck in the yard and wanted to see me. I stood in the hall of Vikki's house and told her that Vikki and I were moving in together and getting married. Zelda's face held a look of shock as she slowly turned and walked out of my life forever. Vikki pointed out that she was devastated. I had not realized the extent of Zelda's feelings for me, or I would have handled it differently. Hurting another soul is probably the worst thing you can do short of murder, and I *hurt* that woman. She didn't deserve to be treated this way. Zelda, wherever you are, you have my sincere and heartfelt apology.

Vikki and I got off to a shaky start, but we stuck it out. Eventually, the boys were grown and gone, and it was just the two of us. We went many places and had loads of good times. She always put me first in her life, and I mostly put her first in mine. After a few years, my fondness for ladies' clothes didn't diminish but got suppressed below the level of consciousness.

When Vikki died a couple of months ago, I started cleaning house. I worked diligently to throw away everything I didn't need in my house— junk, mostly, but there was some stuff I couldn't use and didn't want. I packed up all of Vikki's clothes and took them to Goodwill, only to discover later that I had missed a bunch. I was not very long before I realized I could order stuff online and have it delivered to the house. Sweet. I could pamper myself in a way I never could before—and I did.

I accumulated a nice collection of underwear and started putting together some outfits. This really got started when I found a plastic bin full of clothes Vikki had bought for some of the daughters-in-law. It was maternity wear mostly, but they fit my male frame quite well. They had just enough stretch to accommodate the bulges everywhere. (I am working hard to eliminate said bulges with diet and exercise.) These clothes allowed me to dress properly for the first time in my life. I finally got the courage to venture out of the house in full attire. Although it was scary, I had a blast. I went to dinner and then shopping. Kimberly loves to shop. Richard has always been the kind of guy who goes into a store, grabs what he needs, pays for it, and leaves. That is not at all how Kimberly shops. She likes to take her time looking and trying on clothes, shoes, and accessories, and just being a girl. Understanding some of my female friends' obsessions with shoes and bags and clothes in general is eye-opening, to say the least.

Okay, so we got a little off track again; I'll do that from time to time. Besides my gender identity disorder, I must deal with ADHD, the adult version 1.0. It's untreated. I am not sure if it is real now or just the split personality coming through. Now I really do sound crazy. It really could be that my brain is switching between Richard and Kimberly. (Could that be what is causing the ADHD? I've never considered that before. It seems like a valid theory. I will have to work on some way to prove it out.)

Anyway, back to the point at hand.

Richard is an okay kind of guy. Because he is in touch with his feminine side from way back, he reaches women in a way few other men can. He can understand deep issues and complexities of the female personality. He is a considerate and accomplished lover who is passionate, romantic, sensitive, and caring. He is willing to do almost anything to make sure his partner enjoys each and every encounter, before, during, and after. He doesn't jump up, snatch on his pants, and run out of the house. If you invite Richard over for the evening, you better have some eggs in the fridge, cause one of you is cooking breakfast in the morning, I promise.

Oh, and while we are here, there is another point I would like to make. Men may be from Mars and women from Venus, but men are the romantics. Women love to be romanced, but it is men who are the diehard romantics. Men buy the flowers, chocolates, and Hallmark cards. Women love receiving all of these, but how often does a woman give a man flowers? Some men would like that. Hell, Richard would. But Kimberly absolutely will not send him any. Go figure. Kimberly can be a bitch. I would rather she be sweet as honey, and I will work on that as I build her personality and it evolves.

Richard promised Vikki only two things when he married her: one, that she would never be bored, and two, that he would spoil her to death so she simply couldn't live with anyone else. Richard accomplished both of those promises. For the first six months after the wedding, he bought her flowers every week, to the point that she began to fuss about the expenditure of money and begged him to quit. So he cut back to once a month. In between chocolates and doughnuts and tidbits and trinkets now and then, she died a happy woman and lived a happy life with Richard.

Richard is now winding down his life. Five years and counting till retirement, so for the next few years, Richard must stick around at least at work; I do not think Kimberly has the courage or stamina to fight that battle. I have worked with these people for thirteen years, and I do not think they would react well if I showed up in pink scrubs with makeup on, wearing a bra and a pair of tits. I don't know; they might not give it a second thought, other than to say, "My, you look gay this morning." But I wouldn't bet on it. At this point, they accept gays and lesbians. They are used to that, but we don't have any other transgender people working at the hospital. Well, I don't think so, anyway. Sometimes it's hard to tell. Management would turn a blind eye because of the litigious nature of transgender issues right now; but my work life would be under a microscope, and I would get bounced the very first time I stepped even close to the line.

Richard has been around for such a long time that I simply can't do away with him. Bunches of his better qualities will transfer into Kimberly, I hope, for I have gotten quite fond of the old fart after all these years together. His sense of humor is a must for Kimberly, as well as his sense of honor and duty. I already know that his work ethic will transfer quite nicely, because Kimberly has been working her ass off on the house as she remodels and redecorates to suit her taste. No, we are not painting the walls pink, but we might come up with a mauve comforter for her bed. Or not. Right now, it is olive green with some nice light-green drapes over the sliding glass door. See? Kimberly can decorate—and again, Kimberly is not gay. That's a hard point to get across sometimes.

Richard has had a great life—lots of challenges, lots of hard work, and some good times along the way. He has three great children and the memories of twenty-five years of life with the greatest woman he ever met. Richard has a college education and a great profession and career. As a healthcare professional, Richard's work is very satisfying and rewarding, both financially and emotionally. I remember when life was not so good for Richard, and the only reward he got for completing a task was a couple of minutes to catch his breath from physical labor—and a cigarette before wearily diving back into the pit of hell to try to make it to the end of the day. Not good times there, let me tell you. Life was hot as hell and twice as nasty, and there was barely enough money to put gas in the truck and food in our bellies. Thank goodness that all ended fourteen years ago.

As we reach the end of Richard's life, please know that he goes away happy. It has been a good run, but he is tired and more than ready to turn the reins over to Kimberly for the duration. Vikki's death just took the heart right out of him, and he wants to go find her if he can. He begrudges every second he must spend here and now, when he could be with her in eternity. Neither Richard nor Vikki is overly religious, but they both believed that life survives physical death. Both believed that the spirit or soul lives on. I surely hope so, for both of them.

Buh-bye, dearest Richard. Kimberly loves you with all her heart and will surely miss you.

Chapter Four

Who Is Kimberly?

With Richard out of the way, it is time to start trying to figure out just who Kimberly is. That's not an easy task. Kimberly is in many pieces, each widely scattered across sixty-two years of time. Little bits and pieces of her crop up all over the place, but it's gonna take more than all the king's horses and all the king's men to put her together again. The old gal is quite broken, and I do not think duct tape and super glue will be enough.

Growing up, we watched *The Rocky and Bullwinkle Show*, and we loved Rocky the flying squirrel. One of the segments was called "Fractured Fairy Tales." In this segment, the narrator would tell some fairy tale or other, and it would always have a twist at the end. Every great story has one. Kimberly is a lot like that. I hope her story comes out better than the fairy tales, or at least without the twist at the end.

We already know a couple of things about Kimberly. She loves to shop for clothes. My God, does she ever! I have to keep a close eye on her, or she will spend us into the poor house—but we will look fantastic walking in, that I can promise you. The next thing is, she loves to try on clothes almost as much as she loves to shop for them. Dressing up is so much fun. She loves it all: picking out the perfect outfit, selecting the proper accessories, and experimenting with jewelry. Thank goodness costume jewelry is reasonably cheap, elsewise we would put De Beers over the top. Hell, she doesn't care if it's cubic zirconia or diamonds, just as long as it sparkles.

Kimberly is a class act. Gaudy will not cut it. She would rather have a quarter-carat diamond that looks nice and tasteful than a five-carat rock in a gaudy setting. As a young lady pointed out to Kimberly recently, a little bling goes a long way. She prefers to err on the side of good taste. Understate everything, and let nature take its course.

Kimberly loves to play and shop and have fun. She also loves to work hard and accomplish tasks. Creating something out of nothing is what women have been doing for a long time. Give them sperm, and they will make you a baby. Give them a house, and they will make you a home. Well, Kimberly can't make a baby, but she can damn well make a home.

Work is in progress, I bet you. Kimberly loves to dress up and go out for the evening. She loves it all: dinner and a movie, dinner and shopping, alone or with friends (as soon as she gets some, but that will come in time). The going-out thing has just started, and Kimberly needs a bit of work before we burn too many bridges.

The voice is going to take a great deal of training. Moving like a woman comes along pretty naturally once she gets all dolled up, but even the walk is not quite instinctive just yet. This is all very new to Kimberly. Hey, give her a break! She has only been a woman for a month now. It will take a great deal of time and much hard work and patience to get there, but she will get there.

That is what this book is all about. As time goes by and changes occur, they will appear in text. Maybe the mistakes Kimberly makes will help someone else later. For sure, writing about all of this helps both Richard and Kimberly deal with all of the changes in our lives. We were told not to make major, life-changing decisions following a major trauma. Loss of a loved and cherished mate qualifies as a major life-changing event; I can tell you for a fact. As for the decision? Well, I never really had a choice in the matter, now did I? Kimberly stuck her pretty head up and yelled as loudly as she could, "Is it my turn? Never mind. I am here, and I am not going back into the damn bottle."

Kimberly is here to stay, with or without Richard's consent.

She will not be silenced. She can't wait for me to give her a voice so she can chew my ass out for mistreating her all these years. I predict that she will be a force to be reckoned with as time goes by. She is healthy and working hard to get back in shape and to fit into that bikini by spring. Well, that is what she said. I agreed to lose another twenty pounds, but she wants to drop thirty. She will probably win that battle as well.

Lately, I don't win any arguments. No man has ever won an argument with a woman, and no man ever will. Oh, wait a minute. One man did win an argument with his wife. Then he went to bed. She let him get to sleep and threw the covers over his head and sewed him in. Then she beat the living hell out of him with the broom. Next morning, he apologized quite properly, and they lived happily ever after—but that's just an old folk tale.

As Kimberly begins to learn who she is, Richard will have less and less to do or say about the direction of our lives. For now, we are still together, living in the same body and having fun. In his groundbreaking novel *I Will Fear No Evil*, Robert Heinlein wrote about a man and woman inhabiting the same body. A rich old man hired a doctor to take his brain out of his aged and disease-wracked body and put it into a young person. When the time came for the transplant, the only available donor body was that of a young woman. They both woke up from the surgery and had to learn to live together. Although it is science fiction and a decent yarn, I am now in a similar predicament.

Richard is deeply rooted in my life, and he will not go away quietly. As the cats come over one by one to get petted, I catch myself referring to myself as Papa. The cats do not care about my apparent gender. All they want is a loving hand gently applied in the right direction. It will take a conscious effort of will to change all these old habits. They had sixty-two years to get rooted in my psyche, and they will not be easily banished to the nether regions of my soul. Kimberly will win, and I will end up being the crazy old cat lady down the street.

I have looked at alternative living arrangements. I thought about selling my house and property and moving somewhere more transgender- friendly. UC San Diego is one place I considered, but it is warm there. Seattle has a large LGBT community, but it rains so much (although pot is legal for consumer use there). But moving has a downside. All that packing, leaving friends and family, getting used to a different location, learning my way around. Complications, complications, complications. The last thing I need in my life right now is more complications.

UC San Diego is leading the pack right now. Once I retire, I can move there and live near campus, take college classes on the cheap or for free, and get involved in the academic community and the transgender community there. It's quite large and reportedly very open and safe. Sad that we in this country now have to worry about safety in everything we do. If we live outside the so-called mainstream, we can become victims of hate crimes. Kimberly does not want to be a statistic or an innocent bystander. She wants to live in peace, shop in peace, cook good healthy meals, clean her house, and in general, just *live*. She wants to try on clothes and jewelry and shoes and handbags. She wants to learn how to wear makeup. She wants to go to the theater or a movie. She wants to go out for dinner. She wants to step out for a swim or a walk. That's the lifestyle she wants.

I think one of the things that will come out of Kimberly over time will be the books she will write. This is only the first, I think. Maybe this is the only one she'll write about her transition; I don't know. I do know that she has others locked away, stories that she has been plotting for years while waiting for her day in the sun.

Win, lose, or draw, Kimberly is here to stay.

One day, last week, Kimberly went to dinner and stopped off at a local grocery store on the way home to pick up a few things. On the way out of the store, she almost ran into a coworker who would have blown her cover. That scared her; she's not quite ready to let the cat out of the bag. In a panic, she left her purse in the shopping cart. She drove home, only to find it missing. Kimberly had to turn around and drive back to the store, but, thank goodness, she did recover her purse with wallet, cards, and cell phone. It was somewhat embarrassing to have to explain that the driver's license had Richard's picture on it but that the purse belonged to Kimberly. I have got to figure a way to fix that. I do have a credit card coming with Kimberly's name on it, and that will be fine until I must show my driver's license for identification purposes.

For now, and for the next few years, moving is not an option. So, I will just have to make do with what I have here and learn to live my new life. A very close friend suggested that I should gradually add things from my new life into my old life at work to get my coworkers slowly up to speed as I move from Richard to Kimberly. I guess I had already started to do this when I got my ears pierced. I also started wearing a silver-and-turquoise bracelet that belonged to Vikki. I will soon add another bracelet and then remove the silver one. Little by little, I am letting them see me with my hair down, so to speak. The difference in my appearance is striking, to say the least. Baby steps all, but progress is being made.

As it is late August, and I am out of money for healthcare this year, my facial-feminization surgery (FFS) will have to wait until next year. I have had an eye exam to make sure my cataracts are okay. The doctor said I was several years away from surgery for those, so I can move on with other things. FFS is a *big* step. If I can find a doctor locally who will perform such a procedure, that will be a big bonus. I don't want one who has no experience with this, so if I have to travel to ensure that I work with the right surgeon, I will.

I need a good bit of cosmetic surgery done. I want my nose fixed. I broke it several years ago. It has a bump on it, and it's a bit crooked. I want it slimmed down and straightened. My jawbone is much too heavy and angular, and I need that changed. That is going to hurt, and I am not looking forward to the pain part, but the end result will be worth it, I think. I also want a facelift to tighten the skin a little and iron out the few wrinkles I have there. Who knows? Maybe I can pass as my own daughter. Wouldn't that be a hoot!

There is a major question I will have to have answered before surgery: do I need to have the electrolysis done before the facial surgery? That's something the doctor will have to recommend. Finding a surgeon is the next thing. There are only three plastic surgeons near me, and they don't have privileges at the hospital where I work. Thanks to the HIPAA law, I can be secure in having it done where I work. However, scuttlebutt will spread it all over the hospital. Everyone will know. Of course, when I get my boob job, they are going to figure it out anyway. Unfortunately, I have to get the twins installed before I retire. For one thing, I will certainly not be able to afford them after.

That brings up even more uncertainty. How do I handle this with my coworkers? I think my immediate supervisor would handle it okay. He might not understand it or approve, but he would try very hard not to make me feel uncomfortable about it. I'm afraid the director of imaging won't handle it very well, but the good news is that he is bound by federal law and corporation policy that addresses discrimination.

Come to think of it, I realize I don't know what the policy actually is concerning transgender employees in the hospital workforce. I did a little research: the company does indeed have a policy on gender identity. It specifically mentions sexual orientation and gender identity under the equal employment opportunity policy, which prohibits harassment or discrimination against anyone, regardless of gender identity. Nice. I thought I was going to have to hire a lawyer at some point to enforce my right to work there. Apparently, there are other gender identity disorder people working in the company somewhere. I know I have lesbian, gay, and bisexual coworkers, so it's reasonable to think I also work with at least one trans person, right? If not now, the hospital will have at least one trans person—I say "soon," because it will take a while for all of this to come together for Kimberly.

Tomorrow is a banner day. Actually, today was one also. Kimberly got her first major credit card today. It is on Richard's account, but it has her name on it. Three cheers for good ole Richard. He does have a few redeeming qualities. Anyway, tomorrow, Kimberly gets to pick up her new glasses, some that were made especially for her. To honor Vikki, I had Kimberly's prescription lenses put in Vikki's old frames. They are going to look fabulous, especially with the new pantsuit I bought from HSN.

So, we still do not know who Kimberly is. Her personality is embryonic but growing fast. She knows it will take time. She waits, somewhat impatiently at times, but she waits. It seems that different parts of her will wait for the physical alterations, but that won't begin until 2017, when a host of changes will reinvent Kimberly's life. By the end of 2017, Kimberly will begin to emerge from her cocoon, her butterfly wings still shiny and wet. Hopefully, she will be beginning to look and sound as she should.

I can hardly wait to meet her.

Chapter Five

Through the Looking Glass

"Curiouser and curiouser," said Alice.

—Lewis Carroll, *Alice's Adventures in Wonderland*

At my last session, my therapist said that Richard kept Kimberly sequestered during the last twenty or so years, out of respect for Vikki's lack of comfort with Kimberly—but that is only true to a certain point. Richard did respect Vikki tremendously, as so did Kimberly, but respect only goes so far. The truth is, Kimberly agreed to be sequestered for the duration, out of love for Vikki. It was her love that would not let her cause Vikki any pain whatsoever.

Vikki met me and came to know me as Kim. For all of our married life together, she called me Kim or Kimber. I was the true love of her life and "her" Kimber. She only saw a glimpse of Kimberly, and when she did, she really tried to understand the girl. However, at the time, Richard didn't understand Kimberly very well either.

The Kimber Vikki knew was the personality we now recognize as Richard. He was the dominant one in the relationship. Kimberly was much too immature; she only came out at very limited intervals. She was restricted to a few hurried moments trying on women's clothing and running the dangerous risk of getting caught looking ridiculous. Because of her limited time in the open, Kimberly had to observe and try to develop a personality from the very back rows of the theater. That was a difficult task at best, but Kimberly is a very bright girl.

When Vikki's sudden illness and departure from this plane of existence to the Great Beyond threw Richard into chaos, Kimberly rushed forward and demanded her time. One way or another, she is going to get it. As I stated earlier, Richard is tired and heartbroken from the loss of Vikki. He's ready to move out.

Let me be clear here: neither Richard nor Kimberly is suicidal. Not now, not ever. Richard just knows that his time is up, so Kimberly is taking control. Richard is now (or soon will be) free to go and try to find Vikki, wherever she might be.

When Kimberly finally comes out of the closet (dressed in her best and most fashionable outfit, of course), Richard will be gone forever. He will never surface again. This will take some time, years I think, but as Kimberly comes more to the forefront, Richard will give way and gradually bow out. Just as much as Richard loved Vikki, he also loved Kimberly. It was hard to tell sometimes, because it seemed that he sorely mistreated Kimberly. Again, this was mostly Kimberly's choice.

It will be a relief to have an end to this double life; it's so demanding. As soon as I arrive home from work, I immediately get out of my scrubs and slip into something that is comfortable for Kimberly. I have this fantastic perfume smells so nice, I spoil myself with a little bit when I get home. It would be nice to wear it to work; maybe soon, I can—just a little bit. Maybe my coworkers will think it is one of the patients wearing it. Who knows? We are not supposed to wear cologne or perfume to work because so many people have allergies, but maybe just a dab will be okay.

The big thing is the diet. When he quit smoking, Richard gained fifty pounds and ruined this perfectly good body. So now, Kimberly is working him extra hard to get it off. We are down about thirty-five pounds now and still have quite a way to go to fit into that bikini Kimberly wants. If she starts talking about waxing, I am afraid Richard will put his foot down. Shaving is okay. Kimberly has already shaved her pits and legs and soon her chest. No one wants to see a lady with hairy boobs. Well, Richard might. He has a dirty mind.

Somehow, I get the feeling that Richard is going to stick around just long enough to see Kimberly naked in the mirror. It would just suit the nasty-minded bastard.

It will most certainly be worth the wait. With the weight loss and fitness training, Kimberly is going to be a hot-looking old lady. Once the facial cosmetic surgery is done, the boobs are installed, maybe a little liposuction to restructure the waist area, and possibly a tummy tuck, Kimberly will not look her age by a good ten, maybe fifteen years. The butt does not need a thing. Kimberly has a great-looking pair of legs and a nice tush. The rest just needs a bit of feminization and exercise. So, stick around, Richard; Kimberly will do a little dance for you, you horny old goat.

That is where the *Alice in Wonderland* connection comes in. Carroll's second tale about little Alice was *Through the Looking Glass*. Kimberly will spend a great deal of time in front of mirrors over the next few years, learning how to look, walk, talk, and be a woman. This is not acting class. She will not be acting. This will be Kimberly and has to be natural and instinctive. Alice saw and experienced many strange and wonderful things on the other side of the mirror, and I expect Kimberly will have the same experience.

Electrolysis will end the need for shaving and plucking. The end of shaving is a benefit I am certainly looking forward to. The laser treatments—while not as time-consuming or painful as electrolysis—are not permanent, but electrolysis is. With any luck at all, this will be accomplished by this time next year, and good riddance to the razor (except for the pits and legs, but I think Kimberly can deal with that). Also, I hope to connect with a plastic surgeon by this time next year and start planning the surgeries. We still have to fight with the insurance companies to cover this and this will require a diagnosis of gender dysphoria, as it is called now.

I am not going to feed you the standard line of bullshit that I am "a woman trapped in a man's body." First of all, Kimberly is not trapped. Neither is Richard. They both live here in this meat house in relative peace and harmony. It is almost like Richard and Kimberly are symbionts, each one offering something of value to the other in exchange for living quarters.

Watching the changes come about to Kimberly's body and face will be a marvelous experience, and I can hardly wait for the process to begin. It will have to be after the beginning of next year, so my FSA card will be reloaded. We went through It pretty quickly with Vikki's illness. I also have to find an endocrinologist who will agree to prescribe the hormones and testosterone blockers that will start the transformation. Most of them require a referral from the primary—at least, the insurance companies do.

Only a year or so ago, I asked my primary-care physician for some Viagra. Now I have to go to him and tell him that I want to switch genders. It's okay, I still need the Viagra script, because I still like girls. I can see that conversation going to hell in a hurry. I'll be lucky if he doesn't call the guys in the little white coats to come and take me away to the psych ward. Well, if he does, I hope the guys bring a straightjacket in hot pink. I want the padded room with a view.

The physical changes will be quite striking and will change the look of this body very much. Right now, when in the proper wardrobe, I look like a perverted old fart in a dress. Well, not really. I actually look quite a bit better than some women I have seen recently. I have beautiful hair. It's long, flowing, and snow white with nice curls. The eyes need some work. I have to learn how to pluck my eyebrows to make them look right, but that is coming. I have to have a makeup lesson. Shouldn't there be a high school or college class somewhere that teaches makeup? Once the surgeries start, the cat will be out of the bag. Everyone will know that something strange is happening to Richard.

I have been taking over-the-counter hormone replacements that everyone says works. I do know some women who take these supplements for menopause and swear by them. I do believe that my boobs are getting larger, and sometimes I feel all swollen and bloated. My nipples are a bit more tender and sensitive as well, and it has only been about a month.

I am getting more comfortable in wardrobe and have run into the situation where I stand in my closet and mutter "I don't have a thing to wear." I really have to be more selective in buying outfits. Some tops just don't go with some bottoms. For instance, tomorrow, when I meet with my therapist, I want to go in wardrobe, so tonight I spent about thirty minutes picking out what I wanted to wear. I have two different-size breast forms and still have not made up my mind which I like more: B or C. I will probably go with the smaller, depending on what I look like in the morning when I dress. Richard would never have these decisions to make.

The voice is the next big hurdle. I can deal with everything else out in the world except for that. I have to get serious and start practicing my voice at home. There are plenty of videos on YouTube and other places that will give me step-by-step instructions. There are now new complications with the voice, and now, yet another decision Richard must make.

Richard has had a lifelong relationship with his music. He is a vocalist, guitarist, and songwriter. He says he doesn't play the guitar because he is good at it; he plays because he enjoys it. However, he is fairly good. Richard has a great voice, and over the years, it has gotten much better. He also has a rather large collection of song tabs and lyrics. This past weekend, he connected with someone who may be able to get him a recurring gig at a small venue in Tallahassee, Florida. The one man with a guitar and great songs is the perfect venue for Richard. He doesn't want a lot of money, just a small but appreciative audience. Now the decision comes down to whether he would rather talk like Kimberly or sing like Richard. I am not sure we can do both.

Now, at sixty-two, Richard's music career starts to take off. Why couldn't that have happened thirty years ago, when he was trying so hard? All he does now is play for fun. He also played to entertain Vikki, who loved his music. She was his best critic and helped improve his performances tremendously. That is another part of the loss that Richard has to deal with. Now he has no one to appreciate his music. For some reason, this makes me think of the fortune I got at the Chinese restaurant yesterday: "Keep your feet solidly planted on the ground in spite of what your friends tell you."

So maybe I am not supposed to pursue the music thing. I do know it will complicate things more than a little. Well, I had a thought today: What if I performed as a woman, headlined as the Artist Formerly Known as Richard?

I had some fun things happen today. This morning, I had a session with my therapist, and I had decided to go in femme. What an eye-opening experience that was. As a man, I had no trouble picking out what to wear. If it covered my ass and nuts, it was fine. It just didn't matter what I looked like. Vikki tried and tried to teach me to pick out nice clothes, and she kept me in some nice clothes the last thirteen or fourteen years. We spent a lot of time shopping in Goodwill, and she had a great eye for hardly used men's fashion pieces. I used to get very angry with her the third or fourth time she would send me back to the closet to try again, but slowly I learned. Now that I am a woman, it comes with the territory. Kimberly seems to know instinctively what will work together and what will not. So, we picked out a nice matching outfit, jewelry, and shoes and laid them out for this morning.

Richard used to grumble to Vikki, "Come on, we're going to be late. What's taking so long?" Well, now I know. It just takes a woman longer to get ready than it does a man. Richard could shower, shave, brush his teeth, deodorize, and dress in fifteen minutes flat. Kimberly needs a half hour at best, but forty-five minutes is more like it. There is hair to wash and condition, pits and legs to check and shave (if necessary), powder and deodorant to apply to underarms, and earrings to put in place—and don't get me started about undergarments, which sometimes takes a bit of doing! In Kimberly's case (for now), the breast forms have to be washed, dried, and positioned just so. She has to wrestle with knee-highs or pantyhose as the case may be and get the clothes and shoes on. Takes time, it does. Oh, and by the time you are done, you have to check your hair again, because it is mussed by all the activity with the clothes. Then, don't forget to apply lipstick and any other makeup you may be wearing. Heck, this morning, Kimberly forgot perfume, and she has not started carrying it in her purse, but she needs to.

So maybe being a woman is not all it is cracked up to be, but it's a helluva lot of fun. Because Kimberly looked smashing. We even got pictures. My therapist obviously enjoyed our session today because she seemed more talkative and personable. She commented on how good I looked on more than one occasion, and she dresses well herself. She's very neat and fashionable. I would like to think that maybe she was relating more to me as a female than she did with Richard in previous sessions, because today, I looked like a woman, not a man pretending to be one. One thing that we talked about was how much more comfortable I feel dressed this way than I ever did in menswear.

Although I did a good job as a man, I was never comfortable with the role. It always seemed like I had to try harder to learn the lessons that other men seemed to pick up on the fly. This ties back to the tremendous angst of high school and the first few years after. As I said previously, I was a late bloomer. Perhaps that is because I was supposed to be a girl and had all the skills for that role but had to suddenly learn new lessons in order to fulfill the last-minute role handed to me at birth. The stuff that was supposed to be instinctive behavior, I didn't have.

These are all the things I have learned on this side of the looking glass—the far side, where I am now. I have always heard that hindsight is twenty-twenty. So is looking at the mirror from the back. It was very hard to understand the things I went through as a young man before Vikki died and set Kimberly free. Richard thought he was just slow about social things and sexual things, dating and girls. In some ways, he always was. According to Vikki, women were constantly hitting on Richard, but he never knew it. She would tell him sometimes after the fact that some hussy was hitting on him with her standing right beside him. It used to piss her off something terrible. The claws would come out, and the green-eyed monster would rear its ugly head.

To Richard's knowledge, she never hit one of them, but Vikki could use words the way a gangbanger uses a knife. Damn, she was good.

After the therapy session, Kimberly went to see her friend at the hospital. I took a chance on stepping out of the closet going there, because someone may have seen me and recognized me, and then the pussycat would have been out of the bag—er, closet. We had a nice visit, and I surprised my friend a bit. She was not surprised that I came by en femme but that I looked so good. She took a picture or two with my phone. I had an appointment later that afternoon, so I had some time to kill. I wondered whether to change back into Richard's costume before the appointment. My friend suggested that I go for it and see how it turned out. She said the same thing that my therapist had said: "You look fabulous. Go for it."

So I did. I went to the mall and went shopping for three hours, and I had a ball. I didn't even spend much money, just twelve dollars for two pairs of turquoise earrings. Well, I lost one of the pair I was wearing under a stove in Sears. Damn thing fell out of my ear and slid right under the stove. Try as I might, I couldn't reach it. So, I went down to J. C. Penney and bought two new pairs.

After the shopping, I drove over to the dentist's office and signed in and sat down. In just a few minutes, they called me back, so I didn't have to endure the stares in the waiting room for very long. Then the hygienist called me "mister." Some explanation is required here: this was the same dentist that Vikki and Richard used for several years, so they knew Richard was a male. They had never met or even suspected Kimberly existed, but now they knew.

Once back in the chair, I explained to the hygienist that Vikki had died and that Richard was making some major changes in his life. From now on, he would be Kimberly. She asked if I would prefer that they call me Kimberly from this day forward, and I replied that I would certainly answer to that. I had a nice visit with the hygienist and the doctor. They treated me like a lady and assured me that I was in good hands. I was very open and frank with them about the changes going on in my life, and they were totally nonjudgmental.

Also, for about ten grand, I can get my teeth fixed. While my teeth are okay for a sixty-two-year-old male, they will not work for a sexy female of indeterminate age. They are yellow and worn, and some are missing. So after caps and crowns, some partial plates on the upper and lower jaws, and whitening treatments to remove forty years of cigarettes, coffee, and tea stains, I'll be able to smile again.

As I said, it was a very exciting and fun day. Tomorrow, it is back to being Richard again and back to work, but soon Richard can retire and let Kimberly finish up for him. Besides, she is younger and has so much more energy. Life has not been as hard on her because she was carefully sheltered by her loving Richard. I do hope he sticks around, because we are going to have fun with the rest of this life, and I want him to enjoy it with me.

Chapter Six

"It's a Long, Hard Road"

This chapter title is taken from the song "Long, Hard Road," written by Rodney Crowell and recorded by the Nitty Gritty Dirt Band on the album *Plain Dirt Fashion*.

If one thing is for sure and certain, it's that this is not an easy journey. It's not for the faint of heart. The hormonal and physical changes, the surgery, the new habits to develop, the new wardrobe to buy, and—oh, wait a minute! Strike the wardrobe thingy off the list. That is just going to be plain fun. Kimberly is quivering like an eager racehorse at the starting gate about that wardrobe. Possibly, Richard needs to build on a closet or two for Kimberly before he checks into the nursing home.

These are the obvious things that will take time, energy, money, pain and suffering, and a lot of willpower to accomplish. It is the not-so-obvious things that will cause the most pain and will be the most difficult to deal with. An example of this is my grandchildren.

How do I explain to my seven-year-old grandson that the sweet, old, gray-haired guy he called Papa is now Grandma? I am fairly certain that this will not go over very well. In fact, I am giving serious thought to keeping Richard around a little bit, just for grandkid visits. I could wear a compression band (after the boob job), and the facial changes could be explained off as aging. I will simply dress in some of Richard's old clothes and not wear makeup, lipstick, or nice-smelling perfume.

That is another thing: Kimberly likes to smell nice. She found some sweet-smelling stuff in some boxes while cleaning house. I think they came from Trish, Vikki's sister. She is an Avon lady and was always giving Vikki leftovers and extras that Vikki never wore, but some of this stuff smells wonderful on Kimberly. Even hard-headed old Richard appreciates this stuff. He says it turns him on—to which Kimberly says, "Down, boy, down."

There I go wandering off the main topic again. Back to the children and grandkids. Dan, my youngest son, came up to visit yesterday, and I loaned him my old pickup, as his is down with a bad transmission. He brought my grandson along, and we had a few brief hours together. My son and I had several serious talks about all the things going on in my life, and he went in my (by which I mean Kimberly's) closet to unload the rifles after my grandson, curious as he can be, opened the door and went in.

I am fairly sure that Dan noticed the clothes and especially the shoes. There were a few for Richard and a bunch for Kimberly, some of them still with labels on them from the store. My kid is not stupid, and I bet he thinks he has a pretty good idea what I am up to. Really, I don't think he knows how deep this runs though and how far we will take this. So while I certainly had an opportunity to talk about this with Dan, I'm just not quite ready for that conversation.

Something similar happened on Friday evening. My middle son, Phillip, his girlfriend, Kristy, and I met at a local seafood restaurant. We had a grand time eating, talking, and drinking some beers. I almost told them what was going on. I did tell Kristy that I want to talk to her about me. I reassured Phillip that I was not gay. That seemed to be uppermost in his mind as a concern.

Tomorrow, we are going to spend some time on the creek, and maybe I can tell Kristy then. I have no idea how she will take this, as she has two daughters, one who is seventeen and another who is about nine or ten.

There may be an issue with that. Because at some point, Kimberly could wind up in a restroom with the younger daughter. I do not think Kristy would be comfortable with Kimberly taking her daughter to the restroom. Not that there would be anything wrong with that; I would protect that precious child with my life, and I would never do anything that would harm or embarrass my son's girlfriend or her offspring.

I will have to drive out to Mississippi to tell Thomas, my oldest son. He is the one I predict will handle this the best, because I think he already knows some of it, and the rest he may have guessed. His wife and kids may be a different story. I will leave it up to Thomas to decide what they can handle. I hope to have all this behind me by Christmas of this year. Telling the children is probably the hardest thing I will have to face. The surgery does not frighten me a bit, even though it does have a risk. Telling the kids? That scares me to death.

It is Kimberly's choice to head down this road, and Richard is just barely along for the ride and holding on for dear life. Even though Richard is just a passenger, he is going to throw his opinion in every now and then. Sometimes Kimberly will listen, and sometimes she won't. As I said earlier, Kimberly can be a stubborn bitch.

We have good days and bad ones. Sometimes we pass as female, sometimes we do not. I'm still not sure why that is. Mostly, I think it is attitude and voice. Once I master the voice, I can develop the attitude to go along with Kimberly's personality. I learn new things about Kimberly every day. New pieces of her emerge and shine like new money. This process of forced evolution is a lot of trial and error and of trying to embrace the things that work and discarding those that don't.

The one redeeming thing I have going for me is the dear friend I have found in Tracy. Since I came out to her, she has been nothing but supportive. I try very hard not to monopolize too much of her time, because she has a husband and kids and work—basically, a life. It is a good life that she has, and I am going to be as supportive of her as she is of me. I have another dear friend whom I have come out to. She has some experience with transgender issues, so I hope we can get together and talk soon.

Life is busy right now, and I am finally going to get a weekend off. I think I am on call next weekend, but for this coming one, I am off. Then I work a regular Monday-through-Friday shift. That will be a nice change. I also have booked a motel for the weekend of the twenty-fourth. This would have been my twenty-fifth wedding anniversary. I am going to Okaloosa Island to spend a couple of days at the beach.

I will take plenty of clothes for Kimberly, and her guitar as well. We will see how brave she gets in a crowd of strangers. My plan is to take some scotch and spend the weekend drinking, crying, and playing sad songs on the guitar. Sometimes a girl has to have a good cry, and I have been saving up for this one. Maybe I should pick up a few boxes of Kleenex, because I will need them.

I ordered a new swimsuit for Kimberly; I hope it comes in before we go to the beach. All Kimberly has is a couple of old ones that Vikki left. They fit okay, but they are a bit dated and faded. I probably need to pick up some nice shorts to wear with the swimsuit, though. With Richard's junk hanging down there, it will not be a pretty sight. The shorts will help. The weekend at the beach will be good for Kimberly and Richard as well.

With all the coming changes, I keep hoping that Kimberly will not have to continue taking the antidepressants. The meds work okay, and so far I've avoided the major side effects, but the less medicine I have to take, the better. I think that most of Kimberly's depression was caused by her not being out. In other words, Kimberly was the cause of Richard's depression. I guess it is part of the price we both had to pay to have Vikki in our lives. We pay it gladly, and having Vikki was a bargain at any price.

Once the children know, it will be time to start thinking about coming out at work. This is the main hurdle. Even though I am protected by law, some of my coworkers may not be as open-minded as I could hope. I have one good friend who is very religious. (Well, make that two.) The guy is a Mormon and is pretty traditional. Although, come to think of it, any religion that supports and endorses polygamy should be a bit more open-minded when it comes to gender identity, right?

The other coworker is religious and heterosexual and has a family. I am not sure she will be as open. I hope so. I already know I am going to lose some people from my life, but that is acceptable. If these people can't accept an established fact and accept me as I am, then I probably am better off without them in my life. Besides, it makes more room for new friendships and better people.

My boss is a coal miner from West Virginia. Well, he grew up in coal country, anyway. The man has a master's degree and is super smart, but he may be a bit provincial in his thinking. We will find out before the Christmas holidays. I want to end this year like it began—in chaos. Every few weeks, another train wrecked in my life. The ordinary does not seem to apply to 2016. I hope everything will settle down by New Year's Day. I want to start off 2017 in my new life and moving forward. I never want to look back again, because life is too short. As my dad was fond of saying, "You can't get anywhere new backing up. You only go where you have already been." Oh yeah, his motto was "forward and full speed ahead." Brakes are for people who get into car wrecks. Just an observed fact. At the scene of every car accident, someone has always hit their brakes. Betcha. Of course, by that logic, if we remove brakes from all vehicles, accidents should go down; but that doesn't take into account all the people who don't know how to drive.

Kimberly loves to drive, by the way. She gets into her convertible sports car, and away she goes. It has been too hot for riding with the top down, but that is coming soon. Note to Kimberly: hon, you're gonna need a head scarf to keep all that pretty hair from getting into your eyes. (Update: I just found two scarves in my closet. Kimberly is ready to ride.)

Part of the long, hard road is coming out of the closet. My family and friends must know. This is very difficult because of the emotional impact it can have on these same family and friends. Yesterday, I drove my son to Daytona Beach for a court appearance, and we met with Vikki's sister for a moment at Olive Garden. When my son went to the restroom, I told my sister-in-law. She didn't bat an eye. She may not completely understand, but she is at least nonjudgmental and willing to discuss this openly. I left it up to her to tell her boyfriend. He is a great guy and takes good care of my sis, and I think he will be okay with this.

Trish and I had a nice conversation last evening, after I returned home. She is an Avon rep, and she promised to help me learn about makeup and cosmetics. Of course, she will want to sell some to Kimberly, and knowing Kimberly, she will be a great customer. She also promised to take Kimberly shopping. She goes to good stores. Kimberly is looking forward to this. Somehow or other, shopping with a sister is going to be a great deal of fun, trying on clothes and picking out outfits together. We will have to make a day of it, and Richard better have some big room on the credit cards. He probably needs to get to work on that huge walk-in closet for Kimberly's clothes and shoes.

Again, back on task. The long, hard road also involves the law. There are legalities to be attended to as well. According to the Georgia Department of Transportation, my driver's license can be changed to reflect my gender change, but only after gender-reassignment surgery. Since I am not going to have the GRS done but am going to do the facial feminization surgery, breast augmentation, and a couple of other things to make my body more feminine, I am going to have an argument with the Georgia DOT. I may also hire an attorney to prepare a legal name change. I want to drop Richard from my legal name. Maybe I can get around this by using R. Kimberly Davis. This is indeed my legal name, and no one has to know that the R stands for Richard, right? Heck, it could be Rachel, Ramona, Randi, or Regina, or something similar. So to avoid confusion, with Social Security, the courts, work, and so on, I will just use the R. The driver's license change is important. You need ID sometimes, and it does not help if you are calling yourself Kimberly and the license says Richard.

I had a bad day yesterday. I spent the morning chatting with my brother and his wife. After visiting them, I went to the creek and visited with my son and daughter-in-law. I caught a fish on the way down to the campsite and stayed with them for an hour or so. The Jet-Ski was running terribly, and I barely made it back to the landing. I was very tired. I came back to the house, took a bath, and went to bed. After a couple of hours of rest, I got up and had a fairly good evening.

This morning, I got dressed and went to Walmart for some groceries. I had wanted to make a special meal and needed supplies. Kimberly looked very nice this morning, and things went well at the store. Kimberly is getting better at talking with people, but she still keeps very quiet when in a public setting, speaking only when absolutely necessary. I walk the feminine walk, but I still do not talk the feminine talk—but I'm getting there.

I polished my nails for the first time yesterday. I have redone them twice, and now they look fairly good. It is a learned skill, and I am learning. See, you *can* teach an old bitch a new trick or two. I needed some things from the building-supply store for a chest of drawers I'm trying to refurbish, so I put on my jeans and a shirt, brushed my hair, grabbed my purse, and drove to town—in broad daylight, no less. See, I can pass in the dark of night, especially if there is no moon, but I wondered about daylight. A sweet young lady checked me out and was very kind. As I walked away from the register, she said, "Have a nice day." Of course, I responded, "You too." I got home extraordinarily pleased with Kimberly's behavior. She can be good when necessary.

Things are going well for Kimberly. She is developing a personality and new skills like putting the polish on more than just her nails, fluffing up the core of the new person, and mostly enjoying being who she is. This journey will take much time and effort or her part and an open mind from the people with whom she comes into contact.

This story is as much about Richard as it is about Kimberly. "The Long, Hard Road" is just beginning for Kimberly, but it is ending for Richard. Soon, he will be no more than a ghost in this house, a strong, faithful memory in Kimberly's mind.

Chapter Seven

Open, Sesame

Well, the door to the closet is open. No, silly, not the closet where Kimberly keeps all her beautiful clothes, but the closet door behind which she has been hiding for sixty years. Two days ago, she told just one of her co-workers. Yesterday, she told two more. Kimberly's boss now knows that she is real and will be showing up for work soon. Everyone took it well, and hopefully this will make the friendships at work even closer. That is usually the way it works. Either people look at you in revulsion or the friendships get stronger and closer.

Kimberly realizes that it will take time for everyone to assimilate the changes and hopes that the changes will be gradual enough to allow for everyone to compensate. So far, so good. This may seem a bit fast, and for Kimberly, it is. She was planning to come out next summer or next fall, just before the facial surgeries begin. However, it seems that nature is on Kimberly's side in the timing. The over-the-counter diet supplements she is taking have already begun to work. Her boobs are noticeably larger and still growing.

With this happening, someone is sure to notice sooner or later. Richard is sticking out in places that he should not be. Fortunately, Kimberly is also. So far, wearing loose scrubs and slouching has covered it fairly well, but it is only a matter of time. Soon, Kimberly will have to start wearing a bra to work, and as she continues to lose weight, the scrubs will have to be replaced, and when that happens, the twins are going to pop right out. Surprisingly enough, Kimberly is a bit modest.

When I took off my shirt at the creek last Saturday, I looked down, and there they were—all clean-shaven and standing out proudly. I almost went and put the T-shirt back on, but it was too late. They were out there. The rest of the body sculpting is coming along, although much more slowly. We work out almost every day and continue to watch what we eat, so the weight will continue to drop.

As far as shaving goes, men have a lot more hair on their bodies than women. I have got to do something about that on a more permanent basis than shaving. Shaving all the necessary areas is very time-consuming and can be painful unless you are very careful. I have ordered an IPL hair-removal system that is supposed to work with my skin tone and hair color. The laser treatments will have to be spread out over time, but about four or five treatments in, I should see most of the hair gone from any particular area.

My therapist suggested that I do something about my eyebrows, because they are still very manly. She suggested I go to the mall and have them waxed, which I had actually been considering. I am also thinking I might want to do permanent makeup tattoos on my eyes, as eyeliner and shadowing is tedious and time-consuming. Kimberly may wait awhile on that while she decides which colors and lines need tattooing. There is also the facelift. It would not look good to have tattooed spots on Kimberly's forehead. So, we will postpone the permanent makeup for a bit.

Today is the first day at work since telling my boss. I am sure he will be telling the department director, and I hope he takes it well. Should administration take exception to Kimberly—even though the law and the company's own employee policy prohibit discrimination against anyone for gender identity—there are things they can do to ease Kimberly out the door. This is up to Kimberly. She will have to mind her Ps and Qs, show up on time, and work like hell to be an irreplaceable member of the care team. If Kimberly does not give the administrator ammunition, then they can't fire the gun—or Kimberly.

There are, however, so many coworkers who know Richard, because he does have a happy, infectious personality. Not all of them will embrace

Kimberly as eagerly. The spread of the news about Kimberly will come slowly and (hopefully) peacefully. I still have to tell the respiratory therapists we work with on a daily basis, and they are my good friends as well. Some of this is going to be difficult, and some not so much. All I can do is put the truth out there and hope almost everyone will either understand or at least not condemn me.

The snowball effect will take care of things much faster than I am comfortable with, I'm afraid. It is an exponential expansion and grows at an ever-increasing rate until everybody knows. Most of my acquaintances will be accepting. They may not understand, but they will acknowledge and accept Kimberly. There will be some, of course, who will think I have lost my mind, that losing Vikki pushed me over the edge. There will be some who will forget and call me Richard from time to time. Maybe some will always call me Richard, but I will have to live with that. I will try to overlook the discrimination that is sure to occur and ignore the slurs—up to a point. If they get bad enough, Kimberly will take action. There are rules to this game, you know, and the law now supports transgender people, just as it supports gays, lesbians, and bisexuals.

Saturday, I will work with the fourth and final coworker, Alisha. I will try to have a conversation with her about this. I hope she takes it well, because she is the one coworker whose respect Kimberly wants. There are questions coming from the rest of the team now, and that is the key to acceptance. We got into it just a little yesterday. There were questions about my/Kimberly's voice and how hormones might change the voice. I am sure there will be other questions.

Denise and I have had an interesting thing happen since I told her about Kimberly. It seems that Kimberly and Denise are growing closer together. She is trying to understand and is wondering how Kimberly's sex life will change. Before coming out, and sometime back before Vikki died, Richard and Denise stayed at odds with each other. Richard tried to be civil and work with her as a teammate, but it was sometimes hard for Richard. Denise seemed to be able to piss him off at least once a day.

Since Kimberly's personality has been infusing into Richard's life at work, Richard is much calmer and more relaxed. Denise and I talked about that yesterday.

I think as Kimberly comes more to the forefront, several things will be presented. It seems that a peaceful calm has settled over us, and we are much more accepting of others, as we want others to be more accepting of us. Kimberly has been supportive of Denise and her work efforts and compliments her when she does well. Kimberly has stopped Richard from making negative comments to her as well. I do think that Kimberly and Denise will be great friends yet.

Today marked a landmark day of our "open-door policy." I told my final teammate about Kimberly. I also told a good friend, Mark. I highly respect Mark as a person and a healthcare professional. His wife, Vicki, is a good friend and a nurse as well. Mark and I had a good conversation, and I think he will be okay with the changes. It's going to take some time for all of them to get used to it name change, and I just hope we can make it pleasant as well.

I told my good friend Kara, who works in CT, as well. When I broached the subject with her, there was another tech in the room with us. The three of us had a nice talk. At first, Kara didn't believe Kimberly was serious, because, as she put it, "Richard is a very manly man." If so, Kimberly had a hand in creating the Richard persona. The part about Kimberly not being interested in men and still liking girls is something that is hard to explain—especially because Richard does not quite have that part figured out yet. I also told one of my nurse friends upstairs this afternoon. I think she will be okay as well. So far, everyone has been supportive. Of course, I have only told those who are close to me and the ones I have to work with. More disclosures will come, and surely some people will question my sincerity, motives, and sanity.

Some people will ridicule me, much as they did Caitlyn Jenner. I personally think the Jenner thing was a big publicity stunt and for the money, but maybe not. Far be it from me to question anyone else's motives.

Some people will pull away from me. Some will rally around me. It will be hard to tell which will go which way. There is absolutely no way to predict the responses in advance.

Of course, the old snowball effect is in play here. The more people I tell, the more people they will tell, and soon it will be on the six o'clock news, with film at eleven. I am truly not looking for publicity. This narrative, I hope, will help someone else out there who is going through this as well. Maybe they will avoid some of the mistakes I am sure to make. They'll probably make a few new ones of their own. I do hope to sell enough copies to pay for the publishing costs and maybe a beer or two extra.

Tomorrow, I will have to tell another friend and coworker. This one will probably be the hardest one of all. Luci is so sweet and a true, dear friend. We have worked together for nine years, and although we have had a spat or two, we remain friends. Even when I was mad at her, she was still a friend. I truly hope I do not lose her respect or friendship. That will be a high price indeed for my decision. All actions and decisions have consequences. I just fervently hope the loss of Luci is not one of them. I could never forgive myself if my decision causes her pain. Hopefully, she will be understanding and supportive.

I showed Kara my picture that Tracy took in her office, and Kara was a bit taken aback. She complimented me on the clothes and asked if I picked them out myself. I said, "No, Kimberly did." Kara also stated that had she passed me on the street or in the hall, she would not have given me a second glance.

It has been a few days since I last wrote here. Kimberly has been busy, working and excitedly telling everyone she knows that she is out. I told one of my doctor friends yesterday and a couple of other good friends as well. Everyone so far has been intrigued and has had many questions. All good, of course.

Kimberly is preparing for her weekend trip to the beach. Today she went to the store and bought a couple of bathing suits and a cover-up to wear when she is out and about on Saturday. She picked out the clothes she is taking and got them packed away in a suitcase and valise. Now she only has to pick out what she will wear on the drive to Fort Walton Beach.

At this point, Kimberly is still showing up at work in Richard's scrubs, with Richard's name on his badge. Although my co-workers and friends know about Kimberly, they have not met her yet. While talking with Denise at work yesterday, Richard mentioned that maybe he should bring his travel clothes in and change at work before leaving the hospital. Denise got a bit upset that Richard would even consider changing into Kimberly's clothes at work while patients were in the department and that I should not even consider it. She suggested I should stop somewhere down the road and change. I took this to be highly discriminatory, and the bull-headed part of both Richard and Kimberly would make sure we not only changed in the department restroom but that we spoke to every patient as we walked out!

Personally, I think the problem is that Denise doesn't want to see Richard dressed as Kimberly with her hair down, lipstick on, and—as a friend of mine said Sunday night—with "chin up and tits out." Oh, she left out *ass swinging.* I will discuss this with another of my coworkers tomorrow and decide what I should do on Friday.

I have been slacking off lately on the exercise program, and I have got to get back into the swing of things. I have also not been eating carefully enough, and the weight is not coming off, so I have to tighten up there as well, but for now, Kimberly is holding her own.

Friday is here. I'm at the beach tonight! Kimberly is smiling all the way down to her purple toenails. This weekend is going to be fun, and Kimberly is looking forward to letting her hair down. Things at work are a bit too strained, and it's actually getting worse in my department. Reaction is beginning to set in, and I may get some recoil from the openness. I heard yesterday from a coworker that Denise is talking about Kimberly and Richard in the staff lounge during her lunch break. She does not need to be doing that, as that will get her fired very quickly. My superiors take a dim view of this kind of thing and will pounce on it very harshly.

It seems that Denise thinks Kimberly is moving way too fast and should slow down the timetable. In fact, I think she wishes I would abandon this altogether. I tried to explain to her that I have no interest in changing course and that biology is driving the timetable. She wants me to be Richard at work and Kimberly at home and not go out in public as Kimberly. It makes her uncomfortable for Richard to be "impersonating a woman Somehow, the point escaped her that Richard is well on his way to *becoming* a woman. She is not just playing one on TV.

I had a chance to talk to the CEO and the COO of the company on Wednesday night, and both assured me that they had my back. If I do not have to watch my six, I can move forward. Almost without exception, everyone is cheering me onward. I have the full support of most of the people I have talked to. Some of them think that what I'm doing requires a great deal of courage. Perhaps it does, but "I am woman, hear me roar" doesn't really fit me. I wish for the transition to be over soon, so fewer people will be paying attention to what I'm doing, and more people will just accept Kimberly as a woman. That will come in time, and I predict that I will not take very long.

I am certain that I'll be more accepted after I have my surgery. At that point, everything will fall into place, so to speak. I have to wait until at least the first of the year and talk to my dentist. She may want me to get the jaw and chin done before she fixes my teeth. Kimberly must have a pretty smile, and that is just part and parcel of the same remodeling package she wants. So maybe after the first of the year, we can get the surgery. It will probably take more than one operation. I think it will take four or five different operations for the face alone. Although the surgeon may combine procedures, the jaw and chin and nose are going to be painful as hell. Recovery will be difficult.

I will plan to pick up some scrub tops and try to get my badge early next week. Maybe that will help, because as I start introducing myself as Kimberly, more people will refer to me that way. There will be some who will never call me Kimberly and others who will forget and call me Richard from time to time, but that is okay.

I went into work early this morning so I could catch CJ and talk to her. I didn't want to let her hear about my new gender from someone else. She and I have developed such a sweet, warm friendship, and it is growing nicely. CJ was undisturbed by my announcement, and when I asked her if she would still go on the cruise with me as Kimberly, she said, "Sure, no problem. We'll have fun."

On Friday, I stopped by Walmart and picked up two nice feminine scrub tops and changed into one at the gas station restroom. As soon as I could arrange the time at work, I went to HR and had my ID badge changed to Kimberly. It is, after all, my legal name.

I introduced myself as Kimberly to all my patients, and everything went very well. Then, in the middle of the morning, my department director walked in and asked if he could see me for a few minutes in his office. I followed Reggie to the office. Inside, I saw Brad, the director of human resources, who wanted to talk to Kimberly about her status under the company policy. He assured me that the company wanted to make sure I had a smooth transition from Richard to Kimberly at work and that my job was secure.

He cautioned me about possible recoil from my announcement. Initially, there is excitement and good wishes when you institute a change of this scale. Later, he explained, the initial wave of excitement, curiosity, and support can drop down, and if it does, that's when the negative starts to come out. For a time, there will be negative feedback, but then, the curve starts going back to positive. This is what is called the reaction curve, and it applies when any change is introduced at work. So, I am prepared to receive some negatives. I'm sure that Brad is correct, and I will start to overhear negative comments at some point. One of my nurse friends commented yesterday that she didn't think she was comfortable with my coming out. Should anything negative occur, Brad instructed me to let him and my boss know, so they could handle any corrective action.

The rest of the day went very well, and I received lots of positive comments and congratulations from many of my coworkers. I left early to drive over to Fort Walton Beach for my anniversary weekend with my memories of Vikki. I took a travel outfit in to work and changed in the restroom in the department. No one said a word about this, but I didn't really expect them to.

The trip to Fort Walton Beach went very smoothly. After a nice afternoon drive, I checked in at the hotel easily. The reservations had been made, and Kimberly was expected. I didn't get the room I wanted on the beach; I got a poolside view instead, but that was the only downer the whole weekend. After I unpacked and hung everything up in the closet, I picked out a restaurant for dinner and had a nice time.

Saturday morning, I was up early and went to the beach in my new Catalina two-piece swimsuit. Tracy had recommended a tankini, and that is what I picked out. The bottoms had a bit of a skirt that would hide Richard's junk, and the top fit very nicely indeed. The first time I took off my cover-up, I was very self-conscious. I just knew everyone on the beach was staring at me, but of course, no one was. Some people looked over, as people will, the guys to check out Kimberly's nice legs and butt, and the girls to check out the competition. Of course, once everyone noticed the gray hair, they went back to minding their own business.

I took off my cover-up and quickly walked into the surf. The water was warm, buoyant, and wonderful. After a few minutes floating in the water, I began to feel much more comfortable and a lot less self-conscious. Once I realized that the suit covered enough of my old, fat, wrinkled body, I began to relax. I now have no problem wearing my swimsuit. It feels very natural. I also noticed that my breasts have grown enough that I fill it up fairly well. That is nice. One thing I noticed is that if the top rode up just a bit, some of Richard's belly hair would show through, but I soon fixed that with the razor back in the room.

After a nice morning swim, I returned to the room and took a shower, changed into something nice, and went looking for a nail salon. When I found one, I went in and was greeted by a sweet, young nail tech. I ordered a mani-pedi and a facial. Wow, you girls have been keeping this secret way too long. The leg and foot massage were wonderful. Then we went into the facial room, and that was amazing. I didn't exactly go to sleep, but I did drift off into a deep meditation. This was a most amazing experience.

When the spa treatments were done, I went and found lunch. The seafood, of course, is always great, and I enjoyed it immensely. After lunch and a couple of icy beers, I began to get a bit sleepy. As I'd had a busy morning, I went back to the room and took a nice long nap. About five, I awoke and decided to go grab a swim in the gulf before dinner. Again, the water was so nice that I stayed in for over an hour.

After my swim, I showered and changed and went down to the hotel bar for a couple of drinks. I even ordered dinner in the bar. No one offered to buy me any drinks, but then I was about the only one in the bar most of the evening. After dinner, I made my way back to my room and went to bed for the night. Sunday was going to bring new experiences for Kimberly.

If you're ever in the area, I highly recommend that you treat yourself to Sunday brunch at Harry T's at the Harbor Walk Village in Destin, Florida. The food is excellent and the service beyond compare. The bottomless champagne is nice as well. As soon as the flute was half emptied, the waitress would waltz by with the bottle and top it off. I got looped. About two in the afternoon, I was feeling the champagne quite a bit, so I switched over to coffee and ordered some more food. At this point, I am not sure I could've made the walk to the car, let alone drive back to my room.

An hour or so after the coffee, I felt enough in control to risk the walk and drive. It was a great Sunday, even if it was my last day on the island. I drove back to my room, put my swimsuit on, and with my tablet and bag in hand, I went down to the main pool. The water was a little cooler than the ocean, and although I swam a bit, I mostly laid out on the lounge and read my book.

When I returned to my room, it was nearly dark and getting late. I showered, dressed, and went across the street to have dinner. After dinner, I returned to my room and packed up my clothes and made ready to leave for work on Monday morning.

The drive back to Tallahassee went without event, and it felt good to get back into the routine of work. My peers accepted Kimberly's new appearance without question, and things went very smoothly. Some of the inpatients had questions for me, and we chatted a bit. I received no bad comments, and the patients were very supportive.

After work, I went to the uniform shop near the hospital and shopped for new scrub tops that would appeal to Kimberly's sharp style sense and found a few that would fit. As a guy, Richard wanted drab, colorless clothes that fit his manly appearance. Kimberly, on the other hand, likes nice, warm, bright colors. Print tops look great on her, and she does enjoy shopping for clothes.

The new scrub tops garnered some approving comments and looks from some of the staff. My friend Wendy brought me another top and a pair of scrub pants to try on. The top is a bit small, but will not be for long, as Kimberly is determined to lose more weight before her cruise next spring.

The days went by quickly, and even more people know. I called my oldest son and told him what was happening in my life, and as I expected, he wished me only the best and hoped I would be happy. We had a great telephone visit, and I will get to see him and his incredible family quite soon.

I also told one of my high school classmates. She has been quite accepting. Although she was initially shocked, she got over it rather quickly. I asked her to tell one other classmate, and both encouraged me to attend the upcoming reunion as Kimberly—and I will. There will probably not be another invite after my classmates find out about Kimberly, but that is really not important.

The week went by quickly, ending today. Kimberly has been officially out of the closet for one week. It has been a very exciting and successful week, I think. I am prepared for the backlash that Brad warned me about.

I believe Kimberly is strong enough to handle it. There will be some hurtful things coming, but Kimberly has Richard's quiet strength to carry her though the difficult times ahead.

One thought that has occurred to her is that a thousand people work at the hospital. The chances are very good that there are at least a few more transgender persons employed there. Now that Kimberly has opened the door, maybe they will find the courage to walk on through and join her on the other side. It really is quite nice here.

Chapter Eight

Chin Up, Tits Out

Being "female" is mostly about attitude. Women have a certain walk and presence that immediately says *female*. It is all in the attitude. Women make a strong statement with just that and nothing more. It is more than clothes, nail polish, and makeup. When she found out that Richard was transitioning, Kimberly's friend Susan made a comment on the phone about attitude. Kimberly took her advice to heart: "Chin up, tits out." That just about says it all.

When assuming this posture, Kimberly stands straighter and taller and looks even prettier than usual. Oh, there are better-looking women out there, and she knows it, but Kimberly looks pretty damned good for a sixty-two-year-old broad—especially when she has her chin up and tits out. This chapter will deal with that attitude and how it makes day-to-day living better for her.

She has the clothes, nails, and boobs now. All Kimberly needs is attitude. This will see her though the upcoming rough times. Already there are signs at work that there will be a backlash. At least three people have not accepted Kimberly at face value; they're still calling me Richard. Richard once considered two of these people to be friends. They have not come to terms with the fact that their refusal to call me Kimberly is almost an accusation that what Kimberly is doing is wrong.

The third person is someone Richard has never cared for and Kimberly positively does not like. As the saying goes, he is cordially invited to "go piss up a rope!"

Something that I expected (but didn't expect to happen quite this soon) is that Richard is very quietly fading away. I knew the man was unbelievably weary, but I didn't anticipate him fading away so quickly. I thought it would take months, years even. I know some of him will always be with Kimberly because she takes her quiet strength from the man. She also gets her quirky sense of humor and her happy nature from Richard.

As I was talking to a friend yesterday at work, I could feel Richard slipping away as Kimberly took control of the conversation. Kimberly's eyes misted up, and a lump formed in her throat. I had to say an abrupt good-bye and stumble out the door to get my emotions under control. Some of this emotional instability could be that women are more emotional and the supplements are actually having that effect. I do not know and may never know. I seem to cry a lot these days.

Being out is such a relief. I no longer have to hide and pretend to be someone I am not. I have been surprised at the overwhelming support I get from my hospital coworkers. Every day, I meet more and more people as Kimberly. Some of them have heard that I am out, some have not, but once the initial surprise is over, curiosity sets in and the questions start. What are you doing? Why are you doing this? Are you gay? Will you start to date guys? Are you having your penis removed? Can I see your boobs? Sometimes there are many more questions than answers.

Then there's "How long have you been like this?" At least that one is easy to answer: "Since early childhood." The questions are mostly easy, and mostly I have answers, but sometimes I don't. The questions I can't answer are the very ones that plague me the most. Answers to these many questions will all come in time as this becomes the norm for me.

When I decided to advance the timetable and come out early, there were some things I was not expecting. I do not yet have the wardrobe for this. I am getting there, but not yet. This means that I have to wash clothes a lot. I do not have nearly enough shoes that fit well. That is something I must fix now. I have an event coming up this weekend that will require me to dress nicely, and I only have one pair of sandals that fit. I see a visit to Payless Shoes in my near future.

I ran into my primary-care doctor yesterday. I walked up behind him and tapped him on the shoulder. As he took in Kimberly's attire, his eyes widened in shock, and he smiled.

I said, "Doctor, I do need to see you in the office. We have something to talk about."

He laughed and said, "Yes, I believe we do." He was wearing a gorgeous pink shirt, and Kimberly commented on it. We chatted for a bit, and he will be doing some research to try to help with the change of life. How about that. Sixty-two years old and going through menopause at last. Thank goodness the bleeding stopped. Only kidding, but it is still a time of big change of life for me. The hormone supplements are making some definite changes, and my doctor will need to be in the loop to keep an eye on them. He must make sure that I am okay and not taking something that will harm me later. He also must start thinking about ordering mammograms for me.

Something most people do not know and never consider is that men also get breast cancer. It is rare, but if it does happen, it's just as devastating for a man as it is for a woman. As my progesterone and estrogen levels increase, so will my risk of developing breast cancer. Hopefully, I do not have the gene, but I do not know this for sure. Therefore, I will have to have screening mammograms every so often—another battle to fight with my insurance company.

My weekend nurses on the sixth floor found out about Kimberly yesterday. I went to take a patient back to their room, and as I walked back past the nurses' station, the charge nurse stopped me and asked why I was wearing the pink scrub top. Actually, it was a Care Bears top but nicely feminine. When I explained, she didn't believe me. As we chatted and the other nurses got into the conversation, Antonia came around. Her comment about my breasts was priceless. She asked if she could see them, and I responded in the only way I could think of at the time: "I'll show you mine if you show me yours." What else could I say?

I actually had one of my nurse friends touch them to see if they were real—without advance warning. That was bizarre. I don't mind, as I am not quite used to having boobs to begin with, so having someone touch me on the chest is no big deal, but I can see that it will become one. The nurses on six were very supportive, and we had a nice conversation about what I am doing. They were very sweet about it.

Each day brings new friends and new surprises. I know that sooner or later, I will get some negative comments. I will have to deal with that. The biggest thing is having to remind friends that my name has indeed changed. Some of these people have been calling me Richard for so many years that it will take some time to switch over to Kimberly. I promise to be patient and not get irritated by this, as I do understand the dilemma. Some people will never change over and will continue to call me Richard. I have decided that for a time I will let them, but only for a time. At some point, I will stop answering to Richard. I'll just ignore them until they use my correct name.

As I walked through my first week, chin up and tits out helped a bunch. Every time I would feel self-conscious, I would stand a little straighter, push my boobs out, and hold my head up. This attitude is great. Not only does it help with posture, but it seems to keep people from making rude comments. I know they talk about me as soon as I walk away and that there will be some interesting conversations that I would love to listen to, but I think this attitude will win the day. Most of the comments will be positive.

As I move into week two, I have many things happening this week. Today, I will ride with my middle son to Daytona to go to court. This trip will hopefully resolve his legal difficulties with this event, and he can get on with living his life. Phillip has made some bad decisions in his life. Thankfully, he is starting to make better ones. I hope this turns out well and he does not have to go to prison. Today, I ride with my son as Kimberly. This was a hard decision to make; he and I have not talked at this point. This will be a topic of conversation for us during the six-hour drive. If he refuses to get in the car with me, I may have to come back to the house and change. I hope not.

With the door open, we can have a discussion about what is happening in Kimberly's life. Richard is fading so quickly, and Kimberly is coming to the front. She wants to be out and open and honest—and she is. I hope Phillip will come to see that and not react as a typical redneck American male. I also don't want him to be ashamed of being seen in public with me. That would break my heart.

I heard back from my daughter-in-law the other day. My oldest son finally told her what Papa was up to, and she responded that she was happy for me. I offered to take her for a mani-pedi when I go out to visit them in November, and she was enthusiastic about going with me. We will have a blast.

Once I get back from Daytona, I work for two days and then I'm off for three. My high school class reunion is this weekend. This will be very interesting. As I mentioned earlier, a couple of classmates already know about me; the rest will find out on Friday. I hope they overlook the outside and treat me as they always did. I know they will enjoy the music. Richard will be along with the guitar and songs. Sadly, Kimberly can't sing a note. I think the old girl is tone deaf. So, until she learns to sing, Richard will have to provide the musical end of this show. Kimberly will, of course, provide the costumes. If this does not work out, Kim can always leave early, but I am betting she will have lots of fun and some great visits with old friends. Some of my classmates I have never liked, and others I have missed. It's going to be a great weekend.

I talked to Daniel last night and dropped the bomb on him. He is understandably shocked and does not yet have this assimilated. My comment to him is that I have had all summer to get used to the idea, so it will take him some time. He may never understand, but he expressed his love and continued support for me. We talked at length about exactly what I am doing and how far I am going to take this. He asked if I was like Bruce/Caitlyn Jenner. I said, yes, I am.

The trip to Daytona went very well. Phillip didn't say a word about how I was dressed as we changed cars at his house. He sat there in silence for a bit, and I began to tell him what was happening. By the time we got to Bainbridge, he knew the story. We stopped and gassed up the car, I went into my purse to get my credit card, and Phillip either did not notice the purse, or simply chose not to comment. He did comment about me not saying anything about this at work. I then told him that Kimberly was out at work and everything would be fine there. Times sure have changed. Although more people seem to exhibit violent behavior, maybe society is more accepting of diversity.

So at this point, the entire family knows Kimberly's deep, dark secret. It is not so deep or dark after all. My sons and I all agree on keeping the grandkids in the dark for now, until they are old enough to understand. When I go to Mississippi in November, being Kimberly will be a bit tricky. I plan to take my daughter-in-law out for a spa day with Kimberly. That will be a hoot. I am sure Heidi will enjoy that.

Kimberly is over the last hurdle and is off and running. Well, Kimberly does not run anymore—she strolls sensually, casually along with a big smile on her face, her chin up, and her tits out. The next big event in her life is the class reunion this weekend. This will be a major event for her. Kimberly is ready, almost, and there are things that she will need to do. The first is get her hair done, and that appointment is eleven thirty on Friday. By then, she will have picked out her best clothes and be ready for a nice time. Oh, we must wash the Miata and hope the weather lets us put the top down.

Well, the expected negative response came from Phillip. I got a message from him on Tuesday evening. He commented that he was embarrassed to be seen with me in public and that he was ashamed of my appearance. When we swapped cars back at his house, his stepdaughter ran out and hugged me, but apparently, she had questions about what I was wearing. I just changed cars as quickly as possible and left. I am sure that the child had some questions for Mom and Dad after I left.

Well, this hit me so hard I even thought about stopping this process here and now. I have come out just about everywhere that really matters. My sister and brother will find out eventually, but I will not tell them. I will surely get a phone call from my sister when she finds out.

The point is that I am now being me. I no longer have to pretend to be someone I am not. I knew going in that this would not be all smiles,

Kimberly Davis

laughter, and pretty clothes. There will have to be some learning time for others. I have had all summer to get used to the idea. It will take most of the people some time to assimilate the very drastic changes I am making.

Phillip was supposed to come over on Wednesday and mow my lawn. I had given him a credit card and told him to gas up his pickup before coming over, but when I got the nasty IM on Facebook, I sent him a text. I told him not to worry about cutting my grass and that I would take care of it. I also told him to go ahead and gas up his truck and bring me back my credit card. I also reminded him that I was seriously embarrassed to be seen with him in court with burglars, dope dealers, and thieves, and that I would not let that stop me from being there for my son. His response was that he would be over to cut my grass and everything would be okay.

Phillip came over the next day and mowed my lawn. I had my night-gown on, and he didn't seem to mind. He hugged me and asked for the car keys to move the cars around so he could mow under them. I had cooked a venison stew, and the kitchen smelled great. Phillip asked what was cooking, and I told him. He came in after mowing the grass and enjoyed a bowl of stew. He hugged me before leaving and told me he loved me. I know he does, but he may not approve of my recent behavior. However, given his actions on Wednesday, maybe he will accept Kimberly.

Friday came around, and it was time to go to the class reunion. I had some errands in town and took care of them. I misread the time to go help get the venue ready, so I was a bit late arriving. As I dressed in Kimberly's work clothes for the setup, my classmates were a bit surprised. After the initial shock, they all had questions which I answered as best I could. We were soon busy and the six or so of us worked hard decorating the place and getting the tables set up just so. By the middle of the afternoon, we were ready. I had a few good conversations with my classmates as we worked, but mostly it was work.

After the setup was completed, I raced home to bathe and put on my evening's attire. Kim sure does dress pretty. She went with the print top and the purple pants. We checked on the family members in the path of Hurricane Matthew and found out that they were all okay. No one was hurt, and there was just minor property damage. Dan sent me a picture of Old Red, my antique pickup, to show that it was okay.

I was almost late arriving at the reunion. This was the most terrifying thing Kimberly has done to date. Putting on the two-piece swimsuit and strutting around at the beach was nothing compared with this. With a lump in my throat and terror in my heart, I walked up to the door.

As I approached, I encountered a classmate and her husband. She turned and smiled at me. On Facebook, I had told her that I was looking forward to seeing her and her husband and that we had something to talk about. She complimented me on my appearance and told me to just hang with her and her husband and not to let anyone give me any shit. There were many questions and excellent conversations, lots of pictures of us girls, and everyone was very sweet. There were no negative comments at all, at least within my hearing.

Dinner was served, and it was excellent. The seafood buffet was perfectly prepared and very tasty. Unfortunately, Kimberly does have a guy's appetite and must learn to watch that. She needs to become a picky eater and not put on pounds that take lots of work to remove. There will be prizes for some of us, the usual reunion stuff: Who traveled the farthest? Who lived the closest? Who was married the longest? Who had the most kids? Who had the most grandkids? Who changed the least since high school? Who changed the most since high school?

I am just guessing, but I will probably win the last one, hands down (or should I say *tits out*). I have definitely changed the most. One of my friends wanted to feel my breasts to see if they were fake, and she was nice enough to ask permission. All in all, an interesting evening.

Kimberly went to the second day of the reunion and enjoyed a nice lunch. We worked hard redecorating the hall, and lunch was a refreshing break. I sat with several people I most wanted to touch base with and catch up. After lunch, we went back to the hall and finished the decorations. Later in the afternoon, I went home for a bit and took a nice nap. Well, I'm not eighteen anymore. We old fogeys need a nap now and then if we're going to party like the rock stars we are.

Saturday's evening events were wonderfully planned and executed by the reunion committee. The food for both evenings was the best we have ever had. We had seafood on Friday night, and barbecue on Saturday. Kimberly had to be very careful not to get sauce on her clothes. Now that she must be a lady, everything requires more care. The walk down memory lane was both sweet and bittersweet. We saw old friends and talked about those who were no longer with us.

The reunion ended, and we're all done for another five years. Next up is our fiftieth. I hope I get to be there for that one as well. Maybe with the end of this event, things will slow down for Kimberly and life can get back to "normal." I go back to work today, and that will be a different kind of fun.

As more and more people find out about Kimberly, the going gets a bit easier. After the class reunion, I am more confident in being Kimberly. I look great when I take the time to get dressed. All the little things I do add up. Moving in the world takes a great deal of courage, and I keep hearing how brave I am. Kimberly is becoming more and more dominant as a personality; Richard is fading fast. He will always be there. As a resource, Kimberly can always call on him.

I am no good at painting my nails. I guess that just takes practice, so I will keep trying. I am now wearing a bit of lipstick and powder on my face at work. I keep it plain and not bright. Yesterday, I pulled my hair back into a ponytail, and it worked for me most of the day. Somehow, after I get in the car, it is always nice to pull the scrunchie and let it down.

My boobs are still growing, and now my nipples are getting bigger. I have no idea if they will produce milk, but I doubt it. Stranger things have happened. If the hormone soup I am using convinces my body that I am female and pregnant, they might. Well at least if they do, I'll save on coffee creamer.

When I'm out, it is all about attitude. I am projecting female as hard as I can, and mostly it works; head up and chest out, I allow everyone else to jump to conclusions. The initial excitement is over, and things are settling down nicely. Kimberly is getting more and more comfortable in her new life and enjoying it ever so much.

We have a doctor's appointment next Thursday, when we can discuss hormone replacement therapy (HRT). I realize that I must take in the supplements I am taking and see if the doctor has something better. He has ordered some blood work for me to see if there are any surprises in my system. We will also talk about getting an endocrinologist on board to take over the hormone therapy. I do have someone in mind, but it will depend on my primary-care physician.

While at the beach, I noticed that my right big toe was painful. The nail hurt when I wore closed toe shoes and I realized that I would have to see the podiatrist if it kept getting worse. The week after returning from the beach, I called my podiatrist and made an appointment.

He examined my toe and said the nail would have to be removed. I had that done to the left great toe and the nail bed killed with acid so I do not have a left toenail. Now, I would have a matched set. The doctor set to work and numbed the toe very well. When he removed the nail, I never felt a thing. It would take several weeks to heal and he gave me some wound gel to put on the toe to aid in healing.

I followed the Doctor's instructions to the letter, but it did not seem to be getting better. Two weeks after the procedure, my toe was still painful and red. If it's not better soon, I will have to go to the emergency room. I do not want to have to amputate my toe. It would ruin my look in sandals.

I bought a new cardigan sweater yesterday at Costco, and I love it. It is warm and so Kimberly. Funny, usually Richard loves being cold, but Kimberly wants to be warm and snuggly. The personality differences are still coming out. They will be for a long time to come, I suspect.

I got a check today from one of Vikki's old credit accounts. I don't quite know what to do with it. It is not much, but I need to deposit it into one of the bank accounts. I am still waiting to hear from the VA. I suspect that they are turning me down on her burial allowance. This I will have to fight.

The reality of my decision is beginning to settle in. There are still things beyond my control, but my life is beginning to settle down some. We're having a baby shower at the end of the month for one of my coworkers who is having a baby in January. It just dawned on me today that as one of the girls, I can go to the shower. Now I have to go pick out something nice for a little baby boy. That will be fun. I have never been to a baby shower before. Being a girl is so much fun.

Clothes are still an issue. Kimberly simply does not have enough, but she will get there. I ordered some new scrub tops from Wally World on line, and they will be here soon. I dropped off some pants at the cleaners for alterations. My good friend Renate gave me a beautiful trench coat that only needs cleaning. It has a wool zip-in lining and is very warm. The coat will be the perfect thing for winter outings. Kim still has not made it to Payless Shoes for shoe shopping, but she will.

As the days go by, little by little, people are beginning to accept the changes. I always have to keep in mind that I had a head start of several months on them. The company has announced their annual Christmas party, and Kimberly is definitely going. Now all she needs is an outfit to wear. She has already decided to wear one of her skirts as soon as she can figure out which one. She'll need to buy a pair of nice dress boots. Kimberly is going to be a hottie on the dance floor this year—if her big toe gets well, that is. I absolutely must have a manicure before the party.

To all my gay, lesbian, bi, and trans friends out there, I have some advice: if you have a clash with the religious right, remind them that according to their Bible, God made us too. It also says we are acceptable in his sight. Why, I wonder, do people present half an argument and refuse to present the other half? Is it because it will not support their stand? Some time ago, I said that we need to legalize pot across the United States. After all, it says right there in the Bible that if a man lay with another man, he must be stoned. We only got half the equation right.

Please do not take offense at anything I write. Sometimes I state things as humor that might be offensive to someone or other. Since I live in a glass house, I do not throw rocks. It has been written many times that the cold, hard, factual truth can be offensive to no one—but somehow or other, it does seem to piss a lot of people off.

Truth is sometimes hard to come by, especially in an election year, which this is.

Fact: there are gays, straights, lesbians, bisexuals, and transgender people.

Fact: What I do in the privacy of my home is no one else's business. Not even the government's. When I step out of my home, I have to abide by the rules and laws of polite society. Nowhere in the law does it say what I have to wear or how I have to act. It also does not say how I must have my hair fixed, nails painted or not, makeup on or not—and that is in public. As long as my genitals are covered sufficiently, my ass ain't shining, or my boobs (now that I have some) aren't sticking out undressed, I can parade right down Main Street USA, and no one can do a thing except point, stare, and make rude comments. Freedom of speech is still a part of the Constitution, as is freedom to worship (or not) as we see fit.

Would it not be a hugely boring place to live if we didn't have freedom to be ourselves? We do not have to be little cookie-cutter people who are all the same shape, size, color, and dress. We do not all have to hold the same religious, sexual, gender, or political preferences. There is variety on planet Earth. Wondrous variety abounds and provides us with entertainment for the senses.

As things settle down a bit from the initial announcement and rush, I can relax some and draw a deep breath, thankful that I live in a land where I will (hopefully) not be killed because of who I am, what I believe, or how I am dressed.

Kimberly is out there somewhere, with her chin up and her tits out.

Chapter Nine

And the Doctor Said...

Aside from the mental parts of becoming Kimberly, there are also the physical challenges. First and perhaps the most obvious: I have no boobs, and I do have nuts and a penis. Then there are the hormones and how much of them I have or do not have and what effect they will have on my body. Some of these obstacles can be overcome by surgery, others by artificially adding hormones either orally or by injection. Ouch.

Medical procedures cost a great deal of money. Doctors do not come cheap, and everything they do costs a great deal. For instance, there is one shot that I have been told about that costs roughly $6,000 a pop. Gender-reassignment surgery done here in the United States costs anywhere from $25,000 to $50,000—and that is just the surgeon. There is the anesthesiologist, the nursing staff, and all the other people who work in the OR, and recovery, and post-op treatment, and so forth. All this is like the monkey peeing on the cash-register drawer: it runs into the money.

A boob job (which is going to happen in 2017) runs between $3,000 and $5,000, maybe a bit more. The facial surgery runs between $12,000 and $15,000. The electrolysis to remove unwanted hair is pricey as well. It's about $300 per treatment, and not one cent of this covered by insurance. I have Blue Cross-Blue Shield of Florida, and transgender medical expenses are excluded from the policy. Even though I am protected, by law and company policy, from discrimination, the insurance company provided by my company discriminates against me.

Of course, there are alternatives, such as the over-the-counter substitutes for the hormones I've been taking. Still, they cost me about sixty bucks a month. I can go to Thailand and get the whole surgery package for about US$9,000. This amount includes room and board for two weeks post-op. One quick flight, and two weeks later, I come home minus two balls and a dick, but with boobs and a vagina—and I do not have to qualify overseas like I do here in the States. The only qualification the Thai surgeons want is a stack of paper with dead US presidents on them.

So, the money is an issue. I filed a grievance with the insurance company, and they e-mailed me and then called me. One agent told me that the new year would see changes in the exclusions in our policy that would allow transgender issues to be covered. This was great news. I could keep my rather excellent insurance coverage and would not have to change to a lesser-coverage carrier. With the enrollment deadline looming, I didn't have much time to research this.

Then, a few days later, another agent called me and informed me that the new coverage plan *did* exclude transgender issues. I had to log back into our enrollment website and change my coverage back to the secondary carrier. It's not altogether bad insurance, but they just have a higher out-of-pocket maximum and are 75/25 percent, instead of 80/20. However, the new carrier does cover transgender surgery and hormone-replacement therapy.

I had wanted to do a bunch of dental work and fix my smile. I went to see my dentist, and she did a cost estimate on my mouth. It would cost me about $9,000 to fix everything. I did a double take and started trying to work out the funding. It became apparent that it would not happen in 2016, so I started planning for 2017, but this will take funding away from the transition process, and I am not sure I can do this. I changed my dental coverage from one carrier to the higher-cost one because my dentist would not take the lower-priced one. Later, I reconsidered and decided to find another dentist.

When I bumped into my primary care physician, he told me to call the office and tell them to get me in to see him as soon as possible. It usually takes six months to get an appointment with him, but not so this time.

The next day, I called the office and talked to the appointment desk. They had to juggle a bit but managed to get me an early appointment. The doctor left instructions with his MA to order some blood work and a testosterone level. A week or so later, I went to the lab, had my blood drawn, and was ready to see the doctor.

On the day of the appointment, I went in and was taken back by my doctor's nurse. She, of course, took everything in stride. Tatiana is always smiling and friendly, and I enjoy conversing with her as she takes my blood pressure, temperature, medication list updates, and so forth. She is a sweetie. We talked about the changes that had happened in my life, and she was very supportive. The last time I was in the office, when I was still heartbroken over losing Vikki, I cried a lot. I went through the entire cancer story with Dr. Thacker and cried my eyes out. It was a very emotional time. Now, I am coming into the office as a woman and smiling and happy, and this is a bit strange.

Dr. Thacker came in, and we talked about the surgery and the hormone therapy. He was a bit pissed that I waited till the very end to tell him. He reprimanded me for making him the last one in the hospital to know; he chewed me out a bit, and I began to take offense. He is very difficult to get an appointment with, and I only get to see him about once a year. In between visits with him, should I need medical attention, I see his nurse practitioner.

The doctor asked for a letter from my therapist. He agreed to try to find me an endocrinologist to manage my hormone therapy. I am on my own for a surgeon. There are some plastic surgeons, per my primary-care doctor, who practice in our hospital, so I may take advantage of them for the surgery I need. None of my surgeries are beyond their scope of practice. The facial-feminization surgeries are just routine things like a rhinoplasty, a facelift, a chin bob, and some resculpting of the jawline. Again, these are mostly simple things, but they are costly.

I must wait a few more months for the breast implants. I can schedule that for April 2017, after I return from my cruise. This will give the hormones time to do their magic and grow a set of natural boobs, a process that has already started. After serious consideration, I have decided on a C cup; I think that will be appropriate for my frame. Not too big, not too small. I will not stand out in a crowd, but I will stand out a little. After experimenting with different sizes of breast forms, this is the size that seems to fit me the best.

Dr. Thacker gave me a long lecture on the effects of the hormones I will be taking, particularly the testosterone blocker. The lab work showed my testosterone level to almost at the bottom of normal. Somehow, I knew that would be the case. I have always had enough to function as a male, but not any extra. This balance is what led me here. It let me get away with being male, but it left me with a female side as well. Once the effects of the testosterone go away, I will begin to think more like a woman and less and less like a guy. I think he told me this to shock me, but for me, this is good news. Anything that helps me be more female in thought, word, action, and appearance is good, as far as I am concerned.

There will be physical changes beyond the boobs: the subcutaneous fat deposits will shift around a bit, so gradually I will get more butt (I already have enough of that, thank you very much); my waist will lose some fat and try to curve inward a bit to give me that classic Coke-bottle shape, I hope; and my face will get smoother and more rounded. All these changes will come, but they will need some help. Right now, I am a bit overweight and am working on that. I must get back to my exercise routine so I can tighten up my stomach and help recurve my waist. Besides, the more weight I lose, the better my tits will look.

As the testosterone levels in my body drop, my hair growth will slow down and maybe even stop (at least, that'll happen to my body hair). I will still have to shave my legs and pits, but I hope that the amount of hair on my chest will be reduced. The hair on my chest and abdomen will change from coarse black or gray to a light-blond down. With the hormonal changes to hair growth, I am adding the effects of the pulsed laser treatments, and I believe they are working—maybe not as fast as I would like, but well enough. I have ordered an electrolysis outfit to take care of my eyebrows.

I must drastically alter my diet and exercise routine. Funny, as a guy, I didn't give two hoots in hell about my appearance, but as a girl, I care greatly about how I look and appear to others. This does help me understand Vikki much better, and sometimes, I wish she could be a part of this. I think she might have had fun making me over. Other times, I think she would not have enjoyed it at all. Something about wanting to have a man in her bed. I know it would have been difficult to have been both for her, but as much as I loved her, I would have tried very hard. Had I not been her lover, I think she would have enjoyed me as her friend, but the two were mutually exclusive.

December is here, and Christmas is around the corner. Soon it will be time to start actively recruiting my medical team for the coming year. Of course, I must also deal with the payments on a new car, my new student loan payments, and the routine bills of the household as well. I do have some money budgeted for the coming procedures, and beginning January 1, it will be available to use. I just hope it is enough. Either way, it will go where it will and take me as far as I can this year. If anything remains, we can pick it up in 2018. I think I have enough set aside, but until I talk to a surgeon about the plastic-surgery part, I do not know. I also must work things through the insurance company and hope they pick up enough of this to make a difference.

Once I get back to work next week, I will start looking for a plastic surgeon to take me on. With a bit of luck, I will find one. My problem is I should find a very good one who will work with the insurance company. Most of the time, the surgeon wants to be paid up front. The client must then recover those costs from the insurance company (that usually does not cover cosmetic surgery). In my case, I hope to make a great argument about medical necessity. For me, the cosmetic surgery is about aligning my body image to what my brain wants to see. Mental illness is very real, and when they are unable to restructure their bodies, some transgender people end up suicidal. That will not work for me. I would rather live as I am than end it. Fortunately, I have the means to make the necessary (from my viewpoint) changes to my physical body. The hormones are taking care of the mental tweaks.

There is also down time following the surgeries. I must have enough paid time off (PTO) to cover my paychecks while I am out of work and recovering from the surgeries. The time-away-from-work program will pick up where the PTO leaves off. I will only have to have about forty hours of PTO for each event. I hope to combine surgeries to minimize the number of events in the coming year.

The rhinoplasty must be one event, and the boobs should be another. Hopefully, the rest of the facial surgery can be combined. The tummy tuck and liposuction should be one event. So, I am looking at being out of work at least four times this coming year. This will all be painful to a point, but not overly so. I have learned to simply take it easy until my doctor says I can resume normal activities. My neurosurgeon taught me that when she did the carpal-tunnel release.

Well, there is some good news: the cosmetic surgeons like to combine the breast implant surgery with the tummy tuck and liposuction. The package deal is called a "Mommy makeover." Most of the time, they can do the implants through the same incision they made for the tummy tuck, and that will result in two fewer scars to tend to and worry about. After twenty-four hours, they encourage you to start moving around. Full recovery time is between four to six weeks, at least before a return to work is authorized. The more you can move without lifting or straining the incisions, the quicker you will recover. That applies to almost any surgery.

I have picked out a plastic surgery group that has privileges at our hospital. Now, I must contact them and find out if they can do what I need done—and if they take my insurance. It would be nice to have this done right after the first of the year, say mid-January. That way, I could have my new body for the cruise—but then, the clothes could be an issue. After surgery, some of them may not fit any longer. That will mean Kimberly will have to go shopping some more. Darn it! She hates shopping so much—not! There is also the issue of money for clothes. She simply does not need to spend a great deal of money on clothes that she will need for the cruise. She does have some that fit her now.

Also, recovery may not be quite as complete. We need to be physically active on the cruise. That may be an issue as well, as there is lots of walking, looking, swimming, and physical activity on these things. With all these things considered, I have decided to try to set this up for April or May instead. That will give the hormones time to work their magic, and I will know for sure how big to make the breast implants.

I am tall and broad-shouldered for a woman, so I should have breasts that go with my size. There is a bit of guesswork involved here, as I can't know in advance how much midsection I will lose to the tummy tuck and liposuction. The more midsection I lose, the more prominent my breasts will be. For me, it is not about standing out (well, not too much anyway). It is more a matter of uniformity. I want very much to be generally accepted as a female person. I do not want to be mis-gendered, and that sometimes happens now. With enough teat, that will stop. It is hard for a person to look at a pair of C-cup boobs and say "sir." Girls will automatically look at my hair and clothes and assume that I'm a woman, but guys will look at my boobs first. (Yes, I know it is cliché, but it is a guy thing, something with which I am somewhat familiar.) I have been guilty of the very same behavior. Although I would much rather look at a good set of legs or a nice ass.

The surgeries have been narrowed down from five or six procedures to just two, the Mommy makeover and the rhinoplasty. Procedure wise, I think the former should and will come first. Once I am back at work and have a chance to recover (sometime next fall), I will do the rhinoplasty. I will see my primary-care physician in February, and by then, I will have plastic surgery online, and we can finalize the timetable.

The only other thing I might consider is a facelift. That is an option I will discuss with my plastic surgeon. I do have a few wrinkles; after all, I am sixty-three now. There are droopy bags on either side of my jaw, and

I would like them to go away. I think the facelift and rhinoplasty will fix me right up, and coupled with the breast implants, I will no longer be what's known as a "tweener." A "tweener" is a trans person still in transition. This person has taken part of the journey between one gender and the other but still has attributes of both. My transition will be complete, and the transformation from Richard to Kimberly will be done when the surgery is completed and I have returned to work.

This information is mostly from research that I have done online. I have been as careful as I could be because this involves a bit of risk. For now, this is the plan. We will just have to wait until January and see what the doctor says.

Chapter Ten

The Beat Goes On

Life has progressed, as it usually does. Little happens to slow the progression or change its course. We all march to the beat of the drum; some of us march better than others. I have always had trouble staying in time with the beat. As a man, the beat is somewhat different than the band the females use.

Men learn early on (at least most of them) that they must shower daily, wear deodorant, brush their teeth, arise early, work like hell, play some, generate a substantial income, find a woman, mate, have children, nurture and protect and raise and educate them, put a roof over the heads of the family, food in the pantry, and so forth.

Wait a minute. Hold the bus. Most men just work and generate income, screw their partner, and play. Then there's a bit of beer drinking, hunting, fishing, and any other hobbies that men come up with to distract them from what a helluva thing it is to support and rear a family. The women do the nurturing, childbearing, raising, disciplining, shopping, maintaining the house (dishes, floors, clothes, cooking, cleaning, and so on), taxi driving, bill paying, and all the other hard and/or dirty jobs that no man would do. Most of the time, nowadays, women also hold down a full-time job, generating income as well.

Which raises the question, why do I want to be a woman in the first place? I am already old and unable to have children. That fact alone takes a huge amount of work off the table. Not that I would have shirked it, but I just do not have to perform all those child-related tasks. Besides, I have already raised my three sons, and I was both Momma and Daddy to them for several years. I do have to maintain my house, though, and I find that it is better for me to do the necessary cleaning and cooking and dishwashing as a woman than as a man. Why it is easier for Kimberly to clean house, wash dishes, decorate her new bedroom, decorate her spare bedroom, color coordinate bedding and draperies, I do not know. I just know that it is.

Richard would not have been able to do these things. Not at all. He has no decorating sense, and I worried about that when I started the remodel of the house. When I decided to let Kimberly out to play, she took over the house, and the rest was a cinch for her. With her flair for these things, she did amazingly well. Had Richard done this, it would have looked like a wildcat's ass sewed up with a log chain: it would have been rough. As it is, Kimberly is very pleased with herself and her house, because it is now *her* house, and poor Richard gets to visit on occasion. Kimberly has even considered letting Richard sleep over now and then— but he will have to use the spare bedroom.

I think Richard's visits will come less and less often as time goes by. As pointed out earlier in this narrative, Richard is tired. He just wants to go find Vikki. She is out there somewhere, looking for Richard and hoping he will show up, and he will very soon. Kimberly always sheds a tear for Richard. He is very sweet to her and to everyone he has met, and he is in such pain now.

The drummer keeps pounding out the rhythm of life, and we lemmings keep marching into the sea. Many of us march to a different beat and manage to make a different outcome. Kimberly simply has her very own band and is writing her own symphony. There are a few more like Kimberly out there, and they are beginning to do the same. There is some history within the transgender community, and Kimberly is far from the first to take the journey. Trans people have been around for as long as man. In the early days, most of them hid their difference, sometimes successfully, sometimes not. The more dedicated ones went into acting. It was easier to hide in plain sight. Shakespeare's play, "Romeo and Juliet" was staged in the globe theater with all male actors. At that time, all actors were male and they had to take on female roles which meant wearing the costumes and makeup.

It has only been in recent years that medical science could make the physical transition possible. Prior to these medical advances, transgender persons were sentenced to live out their lives as nature had physically assigned them.

Modern times bring modern thinking, and maybe for the first time in history, transgender people now have a chance at making a life for themselves. Gays, lesbians, and bisexuals have always had a life (albeit sometimes a shady one, but it was a life). Trans people have never had even a little bit of life. For too long, we lived in the closet and never let anyone find out our deep, dark secrets. For many years, we were referred to as transvestites, which is a German word meaning cross-dresser.(Actually the root is Latin, trans, meaning cross, and vestire, meaning clothes or garments. But in its current definition, it came from German.) The underlying physiology and psychology has only recently been established and explored.

The hormone supplements I am taking are working, and I feel more female. The body is changing dramatically, but it takes time. At first, it was a bit strange to go into the ladies' restroom. Now it is strange to go into the men's room. I use whichever restroom I am dressed for. So far, no one has raised a stink, but that will probably happen eventually.

The drummer keeps pounding out a rhythm, and Kimberly keeps marching steadily onward. She called a plastic surgeon's office and made an appointment for January. She is getting very impatient; she's ready to proceed with this next important step in her transition.

Richard, bless his male heart, abused this body somewhat and neglected it shamefully. Of course, Richard did what he had to do to provide a living for Vikki and the family, and that required physical labor and a bunch of it. The results of all that hard work, caffeine, and tobacco abuse is a body that is out of shape and has some health issues. The diet is helping, and the weight has come down, but not quite enough. She still needs to lose about twenty or twenty-five pounds, and with all that weight loss, there must be some exercise to tone everything up.

There are some things that diet and exercise alone will not fix, specifically that soft, sagging skin that looks like a wrinkled potato. For this, Kimberly will need some professional help. Nope, a trainer will not be enough: it's cut-and-stitch time. The tummy tuck, liposuction, and breast implants will be very important to establishing Kimberly's bona fides, and as far as she is concerned, the sooner it takes place, the better.

I talked to my boss today and told him what I had in mind. He said the timing would be okay if I could work everything out with the insurance company and the surgeon. The groundwork has been laid, and the foundation is in, so it's time to execute these carefully laid plans.

As the year ends, I try to focus on the year to come and the promise of a new life for myself at the end of 2017. By this time next year, Kimberly will have been running the show for fifteen months, and only time will tell how that will work out.

It seems as if the tempo of the drums is increasing. Kimberly's best intention was to tread slowly and carefully through this maze of social and medical issues, in the hopes of not stirring up any resentment or hatred or causing any person anxiety or pain. I realize that the haste with which Kimberly has moved into fullness has been upsetting to some. The point to remember is that Kimberly has been waiting for this moment for more than sixty years. I can't tell you how good it feels to be out. I am at the point where I really do not care about what someone else thinks of Kimberly. I just want her to be a safe and happy being—who she is for the first time ever.

The closet is about full, and Kimberly has enough clothes to last for a while. She has plenty for the cruise, nice clothes at that. Of course, after the surgery, there will probably be a need to buy new clothes, as few of the old ones will fit any longer. Yippee. Kimberly does love buying new clothes, but oh, the expense. That can be an issue, and 2017 is going to cost a bundle at best. I am guessing around twenty thousand just to fund the medical expenses. Maybe another thousand or so for clothes.

Kimberly is not a follower of fashion; she is a trendsetter. This comes mostly from ignorance. She sometimes combine outfits in different ways, but the results are smashing. Kimberly does have a great fashion sense and fakes it till she makes it work.

It occurred to me yesterday, while visiting with my friend Tracy as a guy, that I never cared for strip clubs or pornographic literature. I literally did like *Playboy* for the articles. Well, I always like to look at gorgeous women, but the visual side never affected Richard's sexual desire. The girls in the magazines and strip clubs are simply beyond reach, and from Richard's point of view, what's the use of looking at the menu if you can't order an entrée, appetizer, or dessert? Now that I have come to terms with my true gender (female), this begins to make sense. Women tend not to be affected by visual sex acts as much as men are, which is why women wear the war paint and sexy undies and stand in provocative poses. Women want to get laid, and some girls need a guy for that.

Now that Vikki is gone, I can speak ill of her. In her younger days, she very quickly decided that she enjoyed sex. She, genius that she was, concluded that if the boys could be fickle and play with many partners, so could she. Her attitude was, "be safe, but if it's available, do it"—and she did. She had many more partners than I did, but once she settled into a relationship, she locked in and never strayed from her partner. The bed-jumping in her younger days was for fun and experience, and brother, did she have some. She had tried many things, and by the time Richard came into her life, she had boiled it down to a fine sauce. She knew what she liked and what she didn't.

One thing about being a woman is that you can pick your sex partners much more easily. A woman can decide she wants to have sex, pick out a man, and have sex with him. No problem. No man ever turned down the offer of sex. Ever. On the other side of the coin, a man must ask a girl, then suffer the rejection if he gets turned down. Believe me, it takes a lot of courage to put yourself out there like that. Women have the veto power when it comes to sex. They get to choose; and the stupid bitches want equality? No, they do not; women love being placed on a pedestal, just not being left there to collect dust.

Now, there is nothing wrong with this attitude, and some of it is going on today with young, successful, educated people. I find several club runners in Tallahassee who are out to enjoy life and find a sexual partner. Sometimes it's just for the night, and sometimes it becomes a committed relationship. I personally never had a problem with this idea; it was just not for me. I love too easily and give my heart away without thinking.

Sex is not the reason for Richard to become Kimberly. In fact, sex is only a minor consideration for this change. Mostly, I had to decide if I was willing to spend the rest of my live celibate. The number of willing sexual partners for Kimberly just dropped from hundreds of thousands to maybe five or ten. Let that sink in: not thousands or hundreds, but five or ten. As a friend and possible partner pointed out, "What if I don't want boobs in my face?"

My reply? "Get on top."

She laughed, and there still may be some interest there, but I doubt it.

My biggest regret, if any, is that I may not get the time to enjoy being female. Being a woman is a great amount of hard work. It takes some time to learn all the things a girl should know, and most women learn these things as little girls. I never did. Now I must learn my "girl lessons" the hard way, but I am a good student, and I study diligently. However, all the skills I acquire go to making me a better and more attractive woman. I am not trying to attract a man, heaven forbid, but I want to look pleasing to myself and the people I encounter every day.

The march of life never changes, but the tempo seems to be increasing as I age. Now that I have reached this point, I wish it would slow down a bit so I can just enjoy it for a while. Many of you women out there are saying, "Is this person nuts?" No! You all have been women all your lives. I have as well but have not had the opportunity to enjoy it as you have. There are good things about being a female. Nice clothes, better hair, prettier jewelry, and people generally treat you better. Since coming out of the closet on September 23, 2016 life has featured much fun and much hard work, but it's been worth it. My confidence is growing, and my appearance is constantly improving as I refine who I am. I am woman, but I do not want to roar.

I just purr with happiness now and then.

Chapter Eleven

Tits for Tots (or Not)

As 2016 ends, my excitement mounts for the coming year. It will be a very busy one indeed: the first consultation with a plastic surgeon; the cruise in March; surgery in late March (I hope!); then back to work with my new look in May. Oh yes, and more work on the house in the spring. I also need to sell either the timber or land, buy a condominium at the beach, and the list just keeps growing.

As the surgery consult draws near, it is time to start doing research on boobs. There are two different kinds of implants being used these days: saline and silicone. Yes, after the leak scares of the seventies and eighties, the silicone implants are back on the market. This time, they're made of silicone gel and can't leak, even if ruptured. The silicone gel implants can even withstand blunt-force trauma to the chest without causing any leakage or problems.

The saline implants require a much smaller incision, as they are inserted first and then inflated with 0.09 percent normal saline solution. So, recovery time is somewhat reduced. The downside to these is should they rupture or leak, they can go flat on you, necessitating a revision. Who wants to walk around with one nice teat and one flat tire?

If I can arrange the Mommy makeover with my surgeon, there will be only one incision for the tummy tuck and the breast implants. That's only one scar to deal with, instead of three. If done separately, the recovery time for the tummy tuck, liposuction, and breast implants is about four to six weeks (for each procedure). If performed together as one procedure, the recovery time is just four to six weeks for everything. I only pay the anesthesiologist and the facility once. I only pay for one course of the pain drugs. The surgeon will usually give a multiprocedural discount. It just makes much more sense to do this all at once.

The teats will look great but will not be functional. No baby will ever suckle at these boobies. If I have anything to say about it, and I do, no man either. There will be plenty of sensation in them, as I have already discovered. I think the hormones have something to do with this.

Perhaps we had best review a bit of basic biology. We humans (or *Homo sapiens)* are mammals. We give birth to live young and produce milk from mammary glands to suckle and nourish the young until they are well-enough developed to eat solid food. This means until the infant develops teeth. Sorry, "crunchy moms," this does not mean nurse the kid when he is five and attending kindergarten. When the infant's teeth become well enough in place to facilitate chewing, give him something besides your tit to chew on. That's gotta hurt. I have had my finger bitten by a youngster. I can only imagine what one chomping down on a nipple feels like, and I do not want to find out.

The mammary glands we girls are so proud of (or anxious about) depending on the size, shape, and other things, begin as sweat glands. (Sorry, guys, but that is what they are: very specialized and oversized sweat glands.) Instead of sweat, these glands have specialized to produce a milk that is a perfect food to grow and nourish a newborn baby growing into a two-year-old holy terror. Crunchy moms, you should wean your kid from the teat at about the same time you would wean him or her from a bottle. You should start the weaning process at about the time he or she cuts the second or third tooth. By then, you should have the child on cereal, grains, strained veggies, and some meats.

I am not writing a parenting book. There are as many recommendations about this as there are parents, and there are plenty. Everyone has their own opinion. If yours differs from the one herein expressed, so be it. Yours may be just as right as mine. When my oldest was born, the doctor tried to start him on cereal at two weeks. He surely was not ready, and when he cut his first tooth about six months later, he was ready. He jumped at the cereal, veggies, and meats. By his first birthday, we had him eating off the table, and the bottle was beginning to go away. Different kids mature at different rates, and he was no faster or slower than his two brothers.

So, back to the boobies. The time invested in researching options for Kimberly was well spent. These things are not going to be cheap, and Kimberly is only going to get one shot at getting it right. Her boobs must be appropriate to her body—large enough to be noticeable, not big enough to be obscene. Just right. I only hope I can find a surgeon I can trust to give me good advice. I promise to listen and not override him.

Kimberly's boobs will be for show only. They will never be functional in a milk-producing sense, although that may be a possibility with some of the hormones she will be taking. All the hardware will be there, and the hormones may rewrite the software to make milk production possible. Only time and the endocrinologist will be able to tell for sure. I just know that I want to have my boobs look and feel right, and they will. I may be the only one to ever touch them, except for my doctor, but I still want them to be right.

Once the decision is made as to which type of implant to go with, then the biggest decision of all presents itself: how big should they be? The surgeon hopefully will have some input on this and should be able to advise me. I already have some idea about how big they should be, and I will see on Friday what the doctor says. He is also limited to what size implant he can safely fit into the area. The skin will stretch to accommodate several different size. *Teats* are mostly for tots. At least that is the initial design parameter. *Tits* were never meant for grown men, but the puritanism in this country is so rampant that men fantasize about teats. Mostly it is because they were not breast-fed as infants. They remind me of a cat that was taken away from its mother too soon. I have a cat that will dry suckle on a comforter. Grown men do the same thing; it's disgusting. Actually, it's not; it's just a guy thing. Guys just love teats. I know. I used to be a guy, and I love teats. Now, I just prefer that they are my own. Most tits are for tots, but mine are not.

Christmas is behind me, and the new year is looming closer and closer. There will be many new things to do in the coming year and many new things to see. The holidays are about over for 2016, and now it is time to crack down on the diet and start losing weight again. I simply must be below 200 pounds before the cruise and would like to be about 190 by March. I will have to get serious and start working hard to accomplish this. I may even have to go back to Nutrisystem to get back on track.

The more weight I lose naturally, the better the makeover surgery will be. Also, the less fat he must suction away, the cheaper it will be, up to a point. I think there is a base charge and then so much per liter or something like that. I want the surgeon to be concentrating on the tummy tuck and the boobs, not trying to suck out gallons of ugly fat. I also want to look very nice on the cruise, and since the surgery is afterward, I must still diet.

I still think a C cup will be about right for me. That should give me a bust that will be appropriate to my frame and height. I do not want to be in your face with my tits; I just want to look good. I am looking forward to the surgery and not having to wear the falsies any longer. Those damn things start to itch after six or eight hours, and it is difficult to scratch your boobs in public. Guys can scratch their testicles in public. They shouldn't, but they do; but girls can't scratch their teats. Discrimination, it is.

I have been told that you can't feel the implants. I have been told that the breast feels completely natural. I guess I will soon find out. The time away from work will be nice and will give me time to finish this book, but that is months away.

I called to get an appointment with the endocrinologist and was told I would have to wait until May. I may have to try to find another doctor. I had hoped to see a doctor in January, so I could start hormone-replacement therapy before the surgery. My plastic surgeon may insist that I wait for a time before I do the implants, to give the hormones time to work.

I am hoping that he can go ahead and do the surgery, since I have been taking the over-the-counter supplements since mid-July. They seem to have worked very well and are doing what they are supposed to do. I am much more emotional, and I must get that under control, especially at work. One of my coworkers commented on that yesterday.

I tried to explain that the mood swings are more than the hormones alone can account for; 2016 was a very stressful, traumatic year for me. When I returned to work after I lost my wife to cancer, I found out I had to take a $200-a-week pay cut to keep my job. Looking back, I probably should have given my notice at that point and let the company squirm. I tried all summer to get a schedule that would get me weekends off, at least most of the time. I thought I had it worked out in September, but that went quickly south. I ended up working an eight-day stretch every other week, just to get one weekend a month off. It wasn't worth it at all. So, this week I threw down and surrendered. I am going back to weekends full time. That way, I will only have to work five days a week. Hopefully, I can get my eighty hours without having to use my PTO. So, yes, I am a bit stressed. Yes, I am a bit emotional. Yes, I am somewhat pissed off—but it has nothing to do with the hormones, I am telling you (but of course, it does).

Back to the boobs. It seems that breast augmentation has been going on since forever. The first one recorded was in 1898. A surgeon removed a tumor from a woman's breast and used adipose tissue harvested from somewhere else to reshape the breast and fill in the void left by the tumor removal. After that, all sorts of things were tried: string wound up in a ball, gum rubber, paper, glass marbles in a silk sack, saline injections, silicone injections. Most of them failed. In 1963, two surgeons developed a silicone-gel prosthesis that worked well. At least up to the point where they began to leak. After that, there were some problems. Finally, the FDA banned the silicone implants from the market here in the United States.

By then, saline-filled implants became the rage. The saline implants were as prone to leakage as the silicone prosthetics, but the saline would simply be absorbed and cause no permanent harm—but who wants to walk around with a flat tire on their chest? This would necessitate a surgical revision to restore the former glory to the breast. Currently, new prosthetics have been developed that utilize a thicker silicone gel and a tougher envelope to prevent leakage. The new gel implants are very tough. Should the envelope become compromised, the gel stays in place and does not migrate out of the pocket. Also, the new implants have better shapes that make for a much more natural- looking and feeling breast. The new ones also tend to stay put, not rotate or move out of position. It's come a long way, baby.

I have looked at video images about the procedures that I wish to have done. These are serious surgeries. It takes several weeks to recover sufficiently enough to return to work. It can take as much as a year for the scarring to fade to near invisibility. This is not like having a wart removed. I will be a sore woman for a long time.

I think the results will be worth it; I really hope so. For one thing, with bigger breasts, I will be misgendered much less frequently. The tummy tuck and liposuction will also give me a better hourglass shape, and that will also help. The new year just began with me in transition, and I hope the next year will begin with Kimberly—completed.

As time goes by, I get increasingly comfortable with myself and my feminine self. As I always suspected, this is the true side of me, and it feels most natural. The upside of the clothes is that when I dress to go out, I have nice, pretty things to wear. Kimberly may not be a young hottie any longer, but she still looks great.

Sadly, things at work have not progressed as I had hoped. The work schedule has not gotten any better, and I am still working an impossible schedule: eight days straight and two days off; four days on and two days off; and then the cycle repeats. The bad news is that I am not getting my full hours. I must use up my PTO to get my full check and would like to get some overtime occasionally. I have asked to go back to full-time weekends, and I must live with that, even though the company cut my paycheck by $400. I do not think it was right, and my boss didn't stand up for me at all. I can't say too much at work because of my position as a transgender employee. All the company would need is for me to say or do the wrong thing, and I would be out the door. That would solve their "transgender problems" for good, wouldn't it? So far, all issues relating to my gender have been minor. The company has given me full support, as has most of the staff. So, Kimberly dresses and walks differently than Richard. While most of them accept it, some never will be able to deal with it properly.

I took the first step to sell my land and timber this morning. I called my brother and talked to him about it. He was interested, and I may be able to make a deal with him. We are going to look at a timber sale first and then talk about the land later. I still want to buy a condominium in Daytona Beach. I'd also like to pay off the car and the student loans. With the proceeds from a land sale, I might be able to do all three. I think I would like to live out my retirement years in Daytona. The town is a bit more open than Redneckville, South Georgia, where I live now. In Daytona, I can go to the beach, walk on the boardwalk, or explore on Main Street, no one will look or point or say anything.

The LGBTQ community there is a bit better organized, and the atmosphere is more open and accepting. I still must live and work here for the next four years and ten months, but I can handle that. I do have several wonderful friends and a great support network. By purchasing a condominium now, I can have it in the rental program, which nets me 70 percent of the rent. That should make the payments and pay the insurance and homeowners' association fees. Hopefully, by the time I retire, it will be paid for, and I can enjoy my retirement.

So, all that aside, I am beginning to get excited about the surgery and Kimberly's new body. I hope I do not get disappointing news from the doctor on Friday. The new tits are going to be awesome, and I can finally stop wearing these prosthetics. I do not care what they cost; they will be worth it.

Chapter Twelve

What's Up, Doc?

Today, I have my appointment with the plastic surgeon. This will be the first consultation with him, and I am sure he will have many things to tell me. Although I have done much research, there is simply too much information out there for me. Hopefully, the doctor will boil it down and give me the facts I need to make these all-important decisions. Any decision that involves cutting on me is pretty damn important, and I want all the facts I can muster at my disposal.

The appointment with Dr. Kirbo went very well. I was treated well at the office, and even though the wait was a bit long, I finally got in to see the doctor. Dr. Kirbo is a very pleasant young man (well, he's younger than me anyway). He asked how he could help me, and when I told him what I wanted, he seemed fine with my needs. I asked him if he had a problem performing the mommy makeover and he said he had completed these surgeries on several patients and didn't have a problem with them.

I feel much better with this doctor, and I'm glad I won't have to go out of town to get what I need. Once I get the finances in place for the surgery and medical clearance from my primary, I can schedule the surgery for whenever I want. So, I will have everything in place before the cruise and will be able to schedule the surgery for immediately afterward.

According to Dr. Kirbo, my recovery time will be much shorter than I had anticipated. He is talking about maybe two or three weeks before I can be cleared to return to work at light duty. We'll see. I can't be lifting or pulling for the five or six weeks it will take for the scars to heal completely. Scarring will be minimal and will fade with scar care and time and tanning. Yes, I can wear that bikini. Going into the doctor's office was a bit scary, I have no clue why; but after talking with Dr. Kirbo, I am very relaxed and excited over the upcoming surgery. I can't wait to show off my new look.

Bodybuilding is expensive, especially if done by a board-certified plastic surgeon—a little over $10,000. I had anticipated about $20,000, so I feel I'm getting a bargain. As soon as I pay the down payment (10 percent or $1,000), I can schedule the day and time. I will get the medical clearance from my primary next week. Once that's in hand, I'll make the down payment. I wish to schedule the surgery for March 21 or March 22. I must arrange for my son, Thomas to be off that week and come and take care of me. For the first few days, I will be a sick puppy and will need help with the potty chair, food, and so forth.

Because my breast implants will be silicone gel, this will require a somewhat larger incision than the saline implants, but the durability of the gel is far superior. The tummy tuck will have some wound drains left in place for five to seven days. I return to the doctor's office on the day after surgery for an immediate follow-up visit and then back home to rest and recuperate. I will make a big pot of soup or creole food or gumbo, so Thomas can feed me. Or maybe not. That boy can cook, so I may just leave it to him.

I finally spoke with my sister. She is so mad at me that she can't talk. I have heard of someone being "spitting mad" all my life, but I have never witnessed it. My sister was spitting mad. She was spitting the words at me. According to her, I am going to hell for what I've done. She stated that I could never convince her that what I am doing is right.

She told me that she was glad Mom was dead so she wouldn't have to "deal" with this. She said Mom would be embarrassed and ashamed of me. My nieces told her to let it go and let me live as I choose and be happy, but Sis isn't buying it.

I wrote her a letter and mailed it. She should get it today. I unfriended her on Facebook and told her I didn't want to offend her with something that might show up on my page. I also let her know that both Mom and Dad knew about me, that I was the family secret. Every family has at least one, I suspect. I will not answer or return her phone calls and will only respond to a text from her if it begins with "I'm sorry." I suggested she do some research on transgenderism before judging me so harshly. I pointed out to her that her life was not exactly without tarnish and that she had sinned a bit too. Besides, she hasn't been to church in thirty-five years. How does that give her the right to condemn me?

I have made an appointment with my primary-care physician to get cleared for the surgery. I went by the surgeon's office yesterday, made the down payment, and picked up the pre-op paperwork. Things are progressing. I suppose my sister would drop dead if she knew I was having breast implants and a tummy tuck. I don't think she'll be able to stand it. I do hope that whoever "embarrassed" her by telling her about me at least said I was wearing such a cute outfit. Heaven forbid they thought I was wearing ugly clothes!

My brother called. I missed the call but called him back. He informed me that the lawyer would have the paperwork ready for signing and that we could close on the land on Thursday. Steve will be there, and as soon as I have the check in hand, I'll sign the land over to him. That will be a relief in a way. That land has been a thorn in my side for most of my life. I have had it held over my head and been beaten with the inheritance since we bought the place. Now, Steve and Sherri will have it all. It is what they have always wanted, and I can have some investment capital.

I have planned to pay off my student loans and get clear of them and maybe put a large sum toward the car and pay it off early. I will put a large amount into a high-interest savings account, an annual CD or something of the sort. I also have a stock investment that I wish to make and hope for the best. A family friend who was great with money said you should double your investment every seven years. I hope to do a bit better than that, but I will settle for that doubling.

This also gives me the money to pay for the plastic surgery if the insurance does not come through. This morning, I'll call them and start that battle. I am hoping to convince them that this surgery is just as important to my health as cardiac bypass surgery would be. My mental stability and personal body image are very important to my health. I want to look the way I feel, but if I must pay for it, I will.

This has nothing to do with doctors, but I bought a Harley-Davidson motorcycle. Lordy, is that thing fun to ride! I am a bit saddle sore, but it's worth it. I'm having a blast with my bike. It took a few days to get it running right because it had sat unused for several years. My son cleaned out the carburetor, and it's working fine now. Of course, I had to have some new boots—and gloves—and a helmet. I resisted the urge to buy the pink one. I went with white for visibility. Maybe I should look around for a white leather jacket. I am going to enjoy this experience to the max.

My nurse practitioner postponed my appointment for surgical clearance for a week. That is going to take place next Tuesday. I canceled an appointment with my therapist, Lisa on Wednesday. I must contact her and reschedule. Well, everything is rescheduled, and we are getting back on track. Surgery will happen on time and on schedule. I am determined to make everything work out.

The breast implants and tummy tuck will change my physical body forever. However, the surgery will not miraculously turn me into a woman. The physical changes will mark a defining moment in Kimberly's life. This will separate her from Richard.

It is not about "pretending to be a woman" and adopting the body shell to do so. The surgery is about correcting something that happened long ago, when the tiny group of cells started dividing in Mom's womb; maybe even before that. Maybe it's genetic and comes from combining the chromosomes. Science does not know for sure, and I only have a vague theory that I can't test and prove. This surgery is about defining my physical appearance to match the pattern in my brain.

Again, I am not a woman trapped in a man's body. What I am is a bit of both Richard and Kimberly. I do lean heavily toward the female part of my brain, and even the male part of me is a bit feminine.

In my school years, everyone assumed I was gay, but I'm not. My sexual preference is for girls. So, if I am female, maybe that makes me a lezzie. I think that is what I will settle in to be when I finish growing up. Remember, Kimberly has not been let out to play very much in the past sixty years. She is just now going through a very difficult puberty, complete with physical changes and hormonal ones as well. Let me tell you, going through puberty once is bad enough, but I'm going through it for the second time. I do not recall that it lasted this long, but on further thought, I guess it did. Either way, puberty is a bitch. At least I do not have to start a period. That would be just too much at this stage of my life. My surgeon is going to correct my body image and make me look more like the female I feel myself to be.

Already, I am much more comfortable seeing myself as female in the mirror. I do still feel some ambivalence when filling out medical forms. I now check *female* about half the time without thinking about it. I have always hesitated at that question, all the way back to my childhood. I have always had to make a conscious effort to check *male*. When I let my subconscious drive, *female* gets checked every single time. There were clues enough throughout my entire life, but as smart as I am, I was a bit slow on the uptake with this one. I guess I just spent too much time pretending to be male.

The surgical clearance is done and faxed to the clinic. My nurse practitioner is very sweet, and she approves of me and my new look. She is very professional and gave me a thorough exam. I got an EKG and some blood work, and all that info has been sent to the surgeon, so that's one more hurdle jumped. The next step is to get the information for the insurance company, and I will try to do that tomorrow, after I see my therapist. It has been a while since I had a visit with her, and so much has happened.

I picked up the letter from my therapist's office and had a nice, relaxing session with her. It was good to see her after the long break, and there was much news. I told her about my upcoming surgery, and we discussed the ramifications of my new appearance. She seemed relieved that I had decided not to alter my face. I have grown quite fond of this old face, and with a bit of paint and polish, it looks just fine. I am learning how to apply the paint and polish. I'm still finding new things and new colors to try. There are a million of them. Some look good on me, and some don't. Some didn't at first but are growing on me.

I am getting back into my diet, full force. I'm also starting to exercise again. I have some serious work to do before surgery. Dr. Kirbo can only do so much with a knife, no matter how talented he is. I must tone up my core and reduce the belly fat as much as possible.

The money I received from the sale of the family property is dwindling fast. I have two of my sons working on my house. Phillip has poured a new front porch and a new back patio. Now I have a dedicated parking space for the Harley and a place to sit in the front of the house and enjoy a nice evening. The boys are now working on the roof, and at the pace they are moving, it will not take them long. Friday will come soon, and I must pay them. That will use up a big chunk of money. The stock market is doing well, and I have invested the bulk of the funds there.

Sixteen more days, and I can file for my income-tax refund, and that will recharge the bank accounts. This will be the last year I can claim Vikki as a dependent. I will have to figure something out by next April 15, because I am going to owe a shitload of taxes on the land sale—about $21,000, I figure. I had several other projects in mind for the boys, but I may have to table them for now and wait for more money.

The house is finished, and the boys are back home. The change to the old home is amazing. I think we added about $15,000 to the value of the house and only spent about a third of that. I have ordered a pressure washer so Phillip can clean the outside of the house. Once that is completed, the house will be ready for the new me.

Time is moving so swiftly that I can barely believe it. The cruise is less than a month away, and my pre-op visit is only three weeks away. The financing is all arranged, and there will be money enough. Even though I won't be paid for my time away from work, I still must get the leave approved. There is a bunch of paperwork to be filled out and returned to the benefit provider. I have been procrastinating, but I must get this done.

The taxes are done and filed. I will be getting about $6,700 back, and that will recharge the bank. The tax money will help me pay bills while recovering from the surgery and not working. I should have that money in the bank in two to three weeks. I'll also use part of the tax refund to help my oldest son. He is in a bad place, workwise, and he wants to get his CDL so he can become a commercial truck driver. Now is a good time to pursue that because drivers are in short supply. I think he will do well over the road; he loves driving at night, and he's good at it.

I also must help him replace his washing machine. He has seven people in his household, and that requires a lot of clothes washing. His wife has been very sick this year. She has been in and out of the hospital several times since Christmas. Heidi has very bad asthma and is overweight. I am very afraid for her and Thomas. The only way she will survive is to do something drastic and lose the weight. I do love her and worry about both her and Thomas. Thomas is working himself to death, trying to support that family.

I have not been writing in this journal very much lately. Although much is in the works, time seems to stand still, and there is not much actually going on now; but I predict that things are about to begin moving at blinding speed. The recuperation period, following both the cruise and the surgery, will allow things to slow down and give me time to collect my thoughts and put them into the computer. I want to finish this book before going back to work in May. When I go back to work post-op, Richard will be no more, and Kimberly will be in full bloom.

I have been living and functioning as a woman for almost six months now, and it has been highly illuminating. Feedback is just now beginning to trickle in. Not everyone approves. Per my hairstylist, I blew everyone's minds at the class reunion. Apparently, there were many comments. I still have not heard any specifics. I will eventually have to leave this town and move where nobody knows my name. Then I will be whomever I wish to be. I'm working on that. But I must live here until I retire, whether that's in one year or five. The difference depends on which of my plans ripens first.

The big day arrived, and I went to Dr. Kirbo's office for my pre-op visit. The nurse gave me the usual blood pressure reading, took my temperature, and tracked my respiration rate. She listened to my lungs and heart and got a complete list of medications. Of course, she made me undress and put on a paper gown. After the physical measurements were done, we went into a fully equipped photography studio, where she proceeded to take pictures of my chest and abdomen from every angle possible. When the photo session was done, we went back into the exam room. She handed me a bra to put on and then handed me silicone prosthetics. By swapping out the prosthetics, we narrowed the choice down to a five-hundred-gram implant. With both in place, that will add about one kilogram or just over two pounds.

The size looked about right, so that is where I am. After we determined the size of the implants, the nurse stepped out so I could change into my street clothes. I next went into the financial office and paid for the surgery, which went well. I had done some careful planning, and we settled the account handily. The office told me they would call me the day before the surgery and tell me what time to be at the surgery center on Tuesday, March 21. I hoped it would be early because of the length of the procedure.

When I returned home, I checked out my bills and made sure I had nothing pressing for the next few weeks. After all, I'll be on the cruise for a week, and then after that, I'll be in recovery and drugged up post-op for I don't know how long. I wanted to make sure I had left no financial land mines waiting to pop up and blow me down over the next several weeks.

So far, everything is moving according to plan. The cruise is booked and paid for, and the surgery is booked and paid for. I have arranged for the time off from work. I have spoken with the doctor, and the doctor said, "Go for it!"

Chapter Thirteen

A Girl Needs Roots

A quote from the King James version of the Christian Bible says, "for the love of money is the root of all evil." This has been so often misquoted that most people do not recognize the actual text. Everyone says *money* is the root of all evil. I do not believe that is the case. The lack of money can sometimes cause evil things to happen when people try to acquire money, but money in and of itself is not an evil thing.

I have seen people worship money, even more so than their chosen god. The Cajuns down in Louisiana have the best outlook I can think of. They believe that money is something you should spend just before you get it. Personally, I want the last check I write to bounce. I have been to several funerals and have yet to see anyone buried with their money. I knew a couple of people who tried. Did you ever see an armored car in a funeral procession? You won't, either.

I once knew a man who came up poor. He and his brother worked hard every day of their lives. They built up a successful multimillion-dollar business and bought land and built houses for rentals on the side. I did a lot of work for these two brothers. They sold out their main business to their sons and retired.

Well, almost. They bought up more equipment and started another business. They couldn't stand being idle. The older brother finally said he had enough and quit. He stayed home with his wife and played with his grandchildren. The other brother kept working for several more years. He was diagnosed with stomach cancer, and it metastasized. Two weeks before he died, he was on the backhoe trying to put one more septic tank in the ground so he could pocket another $500. His estate was valued at around $80 million. He took not a cent with him.

The point of all of this is money. One of the brothers taught me a valuable lesson about money. He reached in his pocket and handed me a twenty-dollar bill. "Close your hand around that twenty," he said.

I did.

"Now that twenty can't get away from you, can it?" he asked.

"No," I replied.

"But how can any more money get in your hand with your fist closed up tight? You have to be willing to risk losing that twenty to get more."

My friend Shorty was right. Sometimes you must take a bit of a chance if you want to increase your bank account. You still need lots of hard work and careful management. Squandering your resources makes it that much harder to accumulate wealth.

Becoming Kimberly has been expensive. After all, she had to have a completely new wardrobe. Since Vikki died, I have had enormous expenses: first the medical bills, then the funeral, and the loss of revenue from work (something I didn't count on). Then there were all the credit cards to pay and accounts to close out. When the family car died, I decided to purchase a new one, and that meant I also had to go back to full-coverage insurance. Overall, it's been an expensive year so far, and it's not over. The surgery itself will be almost $11,000, plus the money I will pay Thomas to come take care of me for a week. He has a family of seven to support and can't be without the week's income.

I plan to spend a good bit on the cruise as well. I am going to let myself go and enjoy every day and night of the time I spend on the ship and in the islands. I am not going to count the pennies. I'm going to let the chips fall where they may. However, I do not want to end up in bankruptcy. After all, I do have to eat and take care of myself, and someday soon, I hope to retire. So, I have to set *some* limits. (As it turns out, I spent very little more than I had allowed myself on the cruise, but I was still within the budget.)

Money is probably why most couples divorce or break up. If not money itself, it's arguing over money matters that ruins so many marriages. I have heard people say that "money doesn't matter" and "all you need is love," but try telling the grocer that you love him and see how many bags of groceries you walk out with. The same thing applies to the power company, phone company, insurance company, car-loan company, and so on right down the line. They want their money, on time, no excuses. Oh, and heaven forbid you bounce a check. After the merchant charges you thirty-five dollars and your bank charges you thirty-five dollars, the price of that loaf of bread and gallon of milk just went from five dollars and change to seventy-five dollars—and that's if you do not have to go to court too!

So, realistically money *does* matter. In my life, I have had two or three periods lasting a few years each when I had money. I didn't have to budget or think about it because I worked damn hard and got paid well for it. I could buy anything I wanted (within reason, of course). I have had far more and longer periods when I was twenty bucks short of having seventeen cents. Times can get hard when you are trying to raise a family, and for most of that period I had no safety net. There was no one to cover my back.

The boys and I didn't miss any meals, but we came awfully close a time or two. The worst was when we had no food and only four .410 shotgun shells and a borrowed shotgun. My ten-year-old son said he knew where a rabbit was, so I gave him the gun and one shell and told him to fetch. He was not gone thirty seconds when I heard the gun go off.

"Oh, heck," I said, "he missed the damn thing."

Wrong. When I walked out the back door, he came walking up holding that rabbit proudly by its ears. I turned on the Crock-Pot and started peeling taters. We ate on that rabbit for three days, three times a day. Every time the crock would get half empty, I would add more water and vegetables. By day three, there was no meat left, just bones—and they were tender. Best rabbit stew I have ever made in my life.

By the time the rabbit stew was gone, I was working again and got the contractor to give me an advance so I could buy gas and groceries. We were okay for a while. If you have money, it's not important. If you don't, it's deadly serious.

Becoming Kimberly is not without expenses and a bunch of them: wardrobe, shoes, handbags, makeup, hairstylist fees, manis, pedis, waxing, hair removal, nail polish, powder, deodorant, and smell-good stuff. Good perfume is damned expensive, and naturally, Kimberly will not wear cheap shit. Jewelry is another high-dollar item, or it can be. On the cruise, I bought an $800 necklace-and-earring set at Diamonds International at Amber Cove in the Dominican Republic. After I got home, I realized the chain on the necklace was woefully short and will not fit, so I can't even wear the set.

You begin to get the picture. The surgery was $11,000 (plus medications and other post-op costs). There is an ongoing expense for the hormones, one I will have to pay my entire life. Plus, I have my ordinary bills to pay, just like everyone else does. I have been getting large influxes of cash since Vikki died, and I have been trying to pay down my credit-card debt and have eliminated a lot of it. When I finally paid off Vikki's last two credit cards, I called the credit card company to have the accounts closed. The nice lady told me that the accounts had a security benefit, so I got a check back for my two grand.

I have been working on my credit score since I took over the finances last year when Vikki got sick, and I had my score up to over 700 until the surgery. I charged some of that, and so I still must pay those accounts off. Also, the expenses on the cruise were placed on credit cards, and I must pay them down. So, even though my score dropped a few points, I am still good.

The stock investments I have made will either pay off or not. One of them will certainly make me more money than putting that money in a CD or bank savings account. In fact, I am only a few weeks away from getting my first-ever dividend check. The other investment has the potential to make me a couple of million dollars, or I could end up with nothing. Which way it goes depends on the government. I am betting a huge sum of money on this Republican administration being good for business and the economy growing.

Either way, I will be okay. I have never had that kind of money before and will never have it again. My retirement plans are fairly well set, and only the stock market can change that. If the market breaks the bank, I still retire in four years with a comfortable income. I will be sixty-four in November 2017, so I can apply for Medicare next year and drop my workplace healthcare insurance. That will increase my take-home pay. The year after that, I can apply for Vikki's survivor social security and draw that while still working. While I am drawing her social security, I will be increasing my social security check by about 7 percent a year. When I start drawing my own social security at age sixty-eight, it will be enough to live on comfortably and take an occasional trip. Maybe I'll even take another cruise; who knows? Also for the next four years, I am putting 15 percent of my income into my 401(k). So, it is growing again—rapidly.

That is the dark side. The bright side is the economy booms, and Kimberly becomes a little bit rich—enough to be merely "eccentric" instead of "batshit crazy." So, let's explore the bright side for a bit. I will, of course, have to pay taxes on the stock's capital gains; hopefully, that will not be too bad. There should be enough money to take care of Uncle Sam and still not leave me broke. Then I can start shopping for that condominium on the beach in Daytona and spend the rest of my life soaking up "vitamin sea."

Maybe I'll even buy two condos and rent one of them for income. Most of the condominium operators in the Daytona area operate a rental program and take care of everything for 30 percent of the income. That still leaves 70 percent for sweet Kimberly.

With either scenario, once I retire, I am trading the sportster for a soft tail and getting one of those teardrop campers. I'll head out with my bike and see the country on a shoestring. I can always loop back to Daytona and recharge my batteries. Besides, my son and grandson are there, as is my sister-in-law. It will be nice to be in a place where Kimberly does not feel she is being judged. Even though I say I really do not care what other people think, I do a little bit. I think we all do, to some extent. Other people's opinions will not affect my actions, and that is a fact, but that doesn't mean I don't still want acceptance. You may not understand the course I'm following to become female, but you should be able to accept Kimberly as an accomplished fact.

I have always had a hard time with financial planning. Over the years, I have learned and become better at it. It's very hard to tell yourself *no* when there Is money in the bank and you see a pretty dress or pair of shoes. However, you eventually realize that there are limits to the bank account, and you must stay within those limits. Vikki would call me on the way home from work and ask me to pick up this item or that item, and of course, I wanted her happy, so I would do so. Then, when she went to pay the bills, the money would be gone, and she would bitch. "Why did you spend all the money? Don't you know I have to pay the bills?" I only spent the money on what she told me to buy; but the bills still got paid, and since I took over the finances completely last spring, I have been current with everything.

I never want to be dependent on anyone for my upkeep. I have been independent since I turned twenty-one and am completely independent now. I have enough income to offset my expenses and let me save a bit. I have money invested and producing some income on its own. I am still healthy enough to hold down a great job with a decent income. I have purchased some toys for Kimberly, such as the Harley and a Jet-Ski. I now have enough clothes for nights out and shopping. (Not quite enough to suit Kimberly, but enough for now.) I have a new car that will last me for many years and give me great service, and I can keep it serviced on time so it will last. I also have the pickup and the Miata.

So, overall, I am set for a comfortable retirement, one where I will be healthy enough to enjoy some of the great places this country offers and travel a bit. It looks like Kimberly's roots are firmly planted in fertile soil and will grow strong and keep her safe from harm.

Chapter Fourteen

Sometimes It Rains in Paradise

With the pre-op visit to the surgeon out of the way, it was time to start preparing for the upcoming cruise. All the paperwork was in place, and all I needed to do was print my luggage tags and boarding pass. The health certifications were filled out and ready. I cleaned the house, washed all the dishes, cleaned out the refrigerator, filled up the cat bowls with food and the water dishes with water. In short, I tried to be as ready to return home to a clean, healthy environment as possible.

When Richard booked the cruise last June, he had no idea that he would not be going along. Two months later, Kimberly was beginning to emerge and had taken control. After deciding to pursue transition, Kimberly proceeded under the assumption that she would be still in the closet when the cruise took place and that Richard would be the one on the ship. However, as events unfolded, it soon became apparent that Richard was going away, and Kimberly would be out and on the ship.

By January, 2017, it was certain that the cruise would be Kimberly's first big step into a much larger world as a woman. She had no idea how she would be received or whether she would be accepted as female, but she was determined to step proudly into this new adventure. With head high, She walked onto the cruise ship with her friend and her family and hoped that everyone would accept her.

The cruise ship offered plenty of interaction between Kimberly and many of the other guests. At one point, Kathy and I were thought to be lesbian lovers, and Kimberly was accused of treating Kathy badly, by going off on her own, and not leaving a note or saying anything to Kathy. Kathy told me about it after it happened and we both had a good chuckle about this. This was a great indication of how well I was received and accepted as female. For the most part, I was treated as another woman. In fact, I do not recall a single incident when I was not.

We were supposed to leave for Miami on Saturday, March 11, but Kathy had a birthday party going on at her house for her grandchildren. She invited me to come early and enjoy the party, so I did. I had hoped we would be able to leave her house for Miami by around four o'clock that afternoon, but that didn't work out. The party ran long, and we finally got away around five thirty. I did enjoy the party; it was fun. I had known Kathy's daughter, Leeann, from when they both worked at the hospital, and it was good to renew her acquaintance. I did get to meet her brother as well. All in all, it was a nice afternoon.

We finally hit the road and made good time. By midnight, we were only thirty miles from the port, so we stopped for the night. We rented a motel room and got some sleep. No hurry the next morning, as we didn't have to check in at the port until one thirty that afternoon, so we slept in a bit. After checking out of the motel on Sunday morning, we found a Walmart and picked up a few last-minute items before continuing to the ship.

The Port of Miami is huge! It's busy and laid out to ensure the arrival and departure of tens of thousands of people in just a few hours. Rather than drop off our luggage at the terminal, Kathy and I decided to park the car first and hoof it with the luggage to the terminal. That may have been a mistake, but we managed it. I had two huge suitcases, plus a carry-on, plus my purse, plus my small guitar. I managed to stack and wrap everything together so it was not too unwieldy, and we made our way to the terminal. We had arrived an hour or so before our scheduled check-in time and thought we would have to wait. We were pleasantly surprised when the terminal workers moved us right on in and processed us through the security screening very efficiently. Even though my passport has my full name on it, I was still treated by the staff as female. All our bags went through the scanner, and we walked through the metal detectors without a hitch.

We very quickly joined my sister-in-law and her boyfriend, and my niece and her boyfriend. After a quick round of introductions, we were very quickly ushered aboard the Carnival *Splendor*. The *Splendor* is a huge ship. She is 943 feet long, very tall, and carries a whole bunch of people—three thousand passengers and a thousand-member crew.

The gangway deposited us on deck three in an area of the ship called the lobby. As our cabins were on deck nine, we made our way to the elevators and up to deck nine before locating our cabin. Unless you spend a bunch of money on upgrades, cruise ship cabins are damn small. We had an inner cabin with no view window or porthole. Our Sail and Sign cards—your all-purpose ID and charge card while on board—were waiting in the mailbox by the cabin door. We went in, checked out the room, deposited our carry-on luggage, and went in search of alcohol.

We found the bar, got a couple of drinks, and rested for a few minutes before looking around the ship to locate everything. Kathy had to find a smoking place, and the casino was the only inside area where she could smoke. There was a band playing in the lobby, and we soon gravitated back to that area and watched people board. We never felt the ship leave the dock. The departure was so smooth, and of course, there is that mandatory safety debacle you must go through on every cruise ship. They crowded us onto the lifeboat deck at our emergency stations, keeping us there for an hour or more until every passenger had been scanned in. The crew demonstrated how to put on the lifejackets, explained basic safety procedures, and then finally released us. The safety drill is mandated by international maritime law, and the baggage handlers take advantage of the empty elevators and halls to move the luggage to the staterooms. By the time we returned to our cabin, our luggage was waiting in the hall. We had to move it into our cabin and unpack.

Naturally, Kimberly brought a lot of clothes and pretty shoes, just about everything she owned, so it took up a lot of closet and drawer space. Poor Kathy lived out of her suitcase for a week. (Kimberly can be a bitch sometimes. My apologies, Kathy! Next time, you get the closet, and I will use the suitcases.)

There was no affordable cell phone service on the cruise ship, so we had a problem connecting with the family. There is a node on the ship called the HUB which, once downloaded to your smartphone, allows you to text each other, but I couldn't get my phone to accept the download. Sometimes, my phone does that. It is not a true Android or Apple phone, so it doesn't always work with some apps.

By the time we finished unpacking, we were at sea and traveling at a good clip. Our captain kept us moving about twenty knots per hour for the entire seven days. Kathy and I went on deck for a time and then went to dinner. We had chosen the Our Time dining option, and that let us eat pretty much whenever we wanted to. Dress for the first dinner was casual, so we didn't have to get into a formal outfit.

A word about dining on a cruise ship: in the main dining room (or MDR), you will usually be asked if you prefer a private table or not. Kathy and I chose to sit anywhere with anyone. That way, you get to meet other people from different parts of the country. We met several nice couples during the week and enjoyed chatting with them.

Although I got a few strange looks, most, if not all, of our dinner companions accepted me as female. No one was rude enough to comment on it.

We had two "elegant evenings" where the dining hall required us to be in formal attire, and both Kathy and I were prepared. In my new metallic skirt and my new mid-heel shoes, I had the wardrobe to get dolled up nicely for the formal evening.

The food on the cruise ship is everything you would expect it to be. If you see something you like (and you will), order it. They will bring you everything on the menu if you ask. I often had more than one appetizer and entree. The menu changed for each evening, and we always had something on it from each island we visited. There was always something new to try.

Life is short, so buy the shoes. Early on, we decided to try new foods, because we can get regular food at home. So, we tried escargot, oysters Rockefeller, shrimp cocktails, and braised oxtail, just to name a few. One evening, they had a shrimp scampi that was simply the best I have ever had.

After dinner, we went to the lobby to have some drinks at the lobby bar and listen to the band for a bit. We simply fell in love with the Easy Breezy Beautiful Cover Band. They were super and put on a great show every evening. Kathy loves to dance, and when she gets a few beers in her, she's the life of the party. We didn't stay long, as we had had a rather long day and went to bed reasonably early.

Monday was a sea day—all day just riding across the endless ocean, so there was not much to do except wander and smoke. I don't smoke, but Kathy does, and we stuck together most of the time. She wanted to attend the shopping presentation where the sales rep tells everyone where to spend their money. I am certain he is getting kickbacks from the stores he recommends. We bought two coupon books to get free stuff, and we got some nice free stuff. In the end, it wasn't worth the cost of the books, but life is short, and you need to let go sometimes.

On Monday, I had my first little problem with my name. When I paid for the cruise, the cruise line had to have my legal name as it appears on my passport. When they printed up my sail and sign card, they used Richard. When I went to the bar on Monday morning for my breakfast Bloody Mary, the bartender took my card. She then noticed the name and realized that I didn't at all look like a "Dick." She commented that the cards were not transferable. This was a stupendous moment. The bartender actually though I was female and using my husband's card. Priceless. She went ahead and tendered the drink cost as I explained that Richard didn't come on this cruise, Kimberly did.

I knew that I would have to get this corrected or the week was going to be stressful. I went to guest services and met a very nice young lady named Angela. I explained what had happened at the bar, and that I hoped to get the card changed so I would not have any problems getting alcohol. Bless her beautiful heart, she logged into the computer and found my account. Right there on the computer it had all my names. I told her I much preferred Kimberly and that I was desperately trying to get rid of Richard. She smiled at me so sweetly and said it would not be a problem. Within just a few minutes, she had printed me a new card with the correct name on it. My face had so much relief on it that she got tears in her eyes. I thanked her with all my heart. She sent a note to the cabin welcoming Kimberly to the cruise, and every time I would walk by the guest services desk when she was working, I would always get a huge smile and wave. Angela is such a sweet person!

At lunchtime, we went to the buffet on the lido deck, which is on the same deck as our cabin. I was never sure if the main dining room was open for lunch. Turns out it was, and for breakfast as well, but we always went to the buffet. Of course, we took frequent breaks to sit outside of the lobby deck so Kathy could smoke. We met some very nice people out there, and we enjoyed some very stimulating conversations.

Monday night, we connected with the family group and had dinner in the main dining room. We were at two different tables, but they were close enough that we could chat. After drinking most of the day, I was getting a bit tired. We went to the lobby bar after dinner and got cigarettes for Kathy. The band was playing, and we relaxed and enjoyed their set. As we had an early port arrival the next morning and I had booked an excursion, we called it an early evening.

The next morning, I was up at six o'clock and popped out to find some coffee. I let Kathy sleep in. We were due to disembark at our first port of call at seven thirty. I woke Kathy in time for her to grab some breakfast and get ready for the day. The excursion I had booked was a private beach getaway with lunch. We got off the ship, finally, and made our way to the open-air bus that would take us. The drive was about an hour over some of the worst roads I have ever seen. In most places, the road was only a road in the driver's imagination. Caterpillar motor graders and front-end loaders were all along the path, working on the road. At times, we crossed rivers and streams. No, not on a bridge, but through the water and mud. I think the heavy equipment was there in case the big trucks got stuck, but we never did. Not even close. Our driver was very good.

The countryside of the Dominican Republic is very rural and very hilly. Most of it was fenced for livestock (cattle, to be precise), and there seemed to be a great many cattle. Our guide was a sweet lady who was proud of her homeland. The land produced mango, almonds, plantains, and bananas, but mostly cattle.

After being bounced around for an hour, we arrived at Paradise Cove Beach. It was very nice, although the water was not really the clear Caribbean Sea that I longed for. Kathy is redheaded and fair skinned. Needless to say, she and sun do not get along. I found us a couple of lounge chairs with umbrellas in the shade. We bought a couple of beers, and I was ready to get wet. I swam out to a floating platform about fifty yards offshore and just enjoyed getting some sun. The sky was blue, and the sun was warm, and that was just what this old girl needed.

We relaxed on the lounges and watched the people riding the zip lines across the little cove. Kathy sat there and talked herself into trying it. Life is short. It was getting close to eleven o'clock, and we had to eat lunch and get on the bus just after noon. Kathy wondered if we would have time for her to do the zip line, so we asked. We were told we had plenty of time. Kathy paid the twenty-five dollars (United States currency), and they led her off to get harnessed up.

There was a brief training demonstration, and the guides were phenomenal. The took their little group and started for the first tower. My job was to take photos so Kathy could prove that she rode a zip line over the ocean. There was a series of four different lines, and she went over the cove twice. I got the pictures she needed, and while she finished the course, I went to the lunch shelter and grabbed some hot food and cold beer. The food was delicious. Maybe it was the open air or the island cuisine, who knows? It was very good.

After I watched her come across the last line, I started walking back to the harness shed. We walked back to the lunch shelter, and Kathy enjoyed the food as much as I did. After lunch, it was time to board the bus for the bouncy hour-long ride back to the port. All in all, it was a well-done day. We each had fun, we each did what we wanted, and we each enjoyed the day.

Back aboard the *Splendor*, I wanted to shower and change clothes for the evening. While I was getting dressed, Kathy got her shower and then dressed. We headed for the lobby bar to get drinks and relax a bit before dinner.

At no time during this day, was I treated as anything but female. I look female, and am female in every way that counts. This cruise is a major step forward for Kimberly and so far, vindicates my decision to come out of the closet and live true to myself.

I need to relate a word about tipping. Apparently, the cruise lines have had a problem with this, because a 15 percent gratuity is added to everything. Your waiter and his or her helpers, the cabin steward and his assistants, your bartender, and so on right down the line. The tips are part and parcel of the income these people make, and this way, the cruise lines can hire better employees and pay them accordingly. So, with the already-added tip on each drink, you don't need to tip your bartender or waitress, right? Wrong! If you are the kind of asshole who thinks that working for four bucks an hour, seven days a week, for months at a time without a break is a great job with great pay, then do not add anything to your check. You will still get decent service, but only at a minimal level.

With my first drink purchase on board, I added a $1.50 tip, and I did that every single time I ordered a drink. Kathy questioned my action, and I explained that the tip was a little bit extra that I knew would get directly to the people waiting on us. Within twenty-four hours of boarding the ship, every bartender knew Kathy and Kimberly by sight. Most of the time, they even knew what brand of beer Kathy drank, and about half the time, what kind of mixed drink I wanted. The two of us probably got the best bar service of anyone on the ship. I would order a Bloody Mary as soon as the bar opened in the morning, and the bartenders knew just how to make them for me. If we were sitting at a table, our drinks would never get more than half empty before a waitress was stopping by to get us another round.

When I walked into the lobby bar on the fourth morning of the cruise, the bartender was already mixing my morning drink. Being civilized and courteous to other people and treating them with respect is the very best way to get treated the same way in return. I have read somewhere (Facebook probably), that you should treat the janitor with the same respect as the CEO. I disagree. You should treat the janitor with more respect than the CEO, because the janitor works a lot harder for a lot less money and even less appreciation.

Hardly anyone will pass by a janitor cleaning the floor and speak to him. I always try to learn the names of the housekeeping people in my area, so I can greet them by name and tell them how good the floor looks or how well our department was cleaned. It's the same as giving the extra tip. If I need something particular pertaining to housekeeping, I call my friends, and they make it happen. They know I appreciate them and all they do for our organization.

Our next stop was in St. Thomas, part of the United States Virgin Islands (USVI). We docked in Charlotte Amalie. We left the Dominican Republic on schedule and arrived in Charlotte Amalie early on Wednesday morning. We were scheduled to stay for twelve hours instead of the usual eight. Kathy and I went walkabout and shopped for a bit. We picked up some of the freebies and ran into my sister-in-law and her fiancé, so we decided to tag along with them. I had not booked an excursion at this stop, so we could wander about and do what we liked. After some waiting time, we just let the family walk off on their own agenda, and we went off on ours. We rode a cable car up to Paradise Point. We were advised to get the special drink there called the Bailey's Bushwhacker. I had one and ordered some fish wraps and fries. The Bushwhacker deserves its name.

It was frozen, like an Icee, and made with Bailey's Rum. It is an awesome drink.

The view from Paradise Point is breathtaking. You get a broad view of the harbor and the cruise-ship pier. There were three ships docked when we were there. Kathy and I spent an hour up there and then rode back down. At the bottom of the mountain, we caught a cab downtown for some shopping.

We had picked up some maps from the shopping consultant aboard ship and used these as guides. I bought a nice, expensive perfume from the Givenchy store. I absolutely love the way it smells on me. We picked up a couple of freebies, including a Del Sol shopping bag that changes color in the sunlight. I also bought a bottle of nail polish with that color-changing property. It changes from pink to brilliant purple when exposed to the sun. It just warms the cockles of Kimberly's heart. You know how she loves purple.

I found the Harley shop and bought a couple of T-shirts, a coffee cup, and a shot glass or two. I had decided to make the Harley shirts my trip souvenir. The coffee cups I have been collecting for a long time, and the shot glasses were for friends.

After an hour or so of shopping, we decided to head back to the ship. We found a nice cab. The driver was well spoken, and the cab was air conditioned and extremely clean. Kathy and I both commented on this. We had another passenger in the front seat going to one of the hotels on the island, so we got a bit of a scenic ride as well as commentary by the driver. Very sweet lady, she was.

The ride back to the port took a little more than half an hour, and we tipped the driver generously. We made our way down the long pier to our ship, and working through the security stop was very simple. With bar-code scanners and handheld electronics, they scan your Sail and Sign card, get your picture, and record that you are back aboard.

Kathy and I were a bit tired from the walking and a long day ashore, so we went back to our cabin to unload and freshen up a bit. As we were going to be in Charlotte Amalie for twelve hours, the cruise line flew in Chris

Tucker to perform two live comedy shows. As we rested, we decided that we would rather listen to the band and dance than go to the comedy show, so that is what we did.

That night started off quietly enough, with a few drinks at the bar while one of the solo performers played guitar and sang. As it got closer to dinnertime, Kathy expressed that she was not hungry. She decided to just get something from the buffet. I went back to the cabin, dressed for dinner, and made my way to the dining room. Of course, I had excellent table companions and enjoyed great food and good conversations.

When I returned to the lobby bar, Kathy was already getting toasted. The band we loved came on and started playing some great dance music. Kathy is not shy. She would see someone patting his foot to the music and would go grab him and lead him onto the floor. Before she was through, we had the dance floor full, and the crowd was loving it.

Sometime during the evening, Betta and Terry, two young ladies we met one night at dinner, joined us. Kathy talked them into sitting with us and dancing as well—but we had to promise to go to the line dance on the ninth deck just aft of our cabin. Our lead singer found a little three-year-old toddler and was teaching her to dance while singing. Talented young lady, that one.

At some point during the evening (I must have been in the restroom), Kathy lost her balance and fell flat on her butt. She laughed and told me the next morning that she broke her butt. I think she just bruised it, but she slept in. I'm not sure she even got off the boat at our next port of call.

Our third island stop was in San Juan, Puerto Rico. After we arrived there about eight thirty on Thursday morning, I got geared up and went walkabout. There were street venders all along the harbor road on the excellent sidewalks. However, I was looking for a restaurant that the band singer had recommended to me. It was a place called Raices in Old San Juan, and she told me they had great mofongo, the national dish. She also recommended the fried pork chop.

As I was searching for this place, I found the San Juan Harley shop. I went in, bought my T-shirt and coffee cup, and picked up an extra T-shirt for Kathy's son, Derek. The clerk in the store told me how to find the restaurant. I walked out of the Harley shop and up two long fights of steps and found myself on a quiet little street in Old Town. The stores and shops were painted bright, sunny colors, and the street was very pretty. I made my way to the restaurant, but it had not opened yet. There was a shaded bench out front, so I sat myself down and just enjoyed the surroundings.

There was an hour wait until opening time, and the quaint little street was nice. The pedestrians on the sidewalk moved along with purpose, and it was quite simple to separate the islanders from the visitors. The islanders all dressed like people in the States when going about their routine affairs. The visitors brought bright, island-colored shorts and shirts; most wore sandals or flip-flops; and they all carried a backpack or shopping bag.

The restaurant finally opened, and I was seated and given a menu. Everything on it was mouthwatering. I followed my friend's recommendation and ordered a mojito and the mofongo with the fried pork chop.

When the waitress brought my platter. It had the biggest pork chop I have ever seen. It must have come from a hog the size of a small cow. The mojito was the best I have ever had, and I can't tell you how good the pork chop was. Mofongo is made from green plantains mashed up in a pestle and mixed with liquid. It is a little bland, and it is more like a potato dish here in the States, but it went with the pork chop and salad extremely well. I managed to consume about a third of the chop, mofongo, and salad.

After settling my check, I headed back to the ship. As I walked along the street, I started passing the street vendors again. I stopped and bought two shot glasses. I stopped at another booth whose owner made wind chimes out of wine bottles and seashells. I bought one for my good friend. We packed it carefully—or so we thought. Later, back at home, when my friend opened the package, it was broken.

I made my way back through customs and walked through the huge warehouse to finally reach the gangway and board the ship. I went up to the room, and Kathy was just waking up. I unpacked my goodies and gave her the shirt I had purchased for her son. She wanted to go out and smoke, so I waited for her to get dressed. We then made our way to the smoking area on deck three.

While she was smoking, the ship left port, and we slowly backed away from the pier. With the harbor pilot onboard, the *Splendor* made its way out of San Juan Harbor. Just before leaving the harbor and entering open sea, the pilot boat moved in close to the side of the ship, and the harbor pilot transferred from the *Splendor* to the pilot boat. I'm not sure that I would want to try that, but they do this nearly every day. I understand that there are seldom mishaps while accomplishing this maneuver.

Although Kathy was sore from her fall, we stopped in at the bar and listened to the music for a while. This was the second elegant night in the dining room, but neither of us wanted to get all dolled up just for dinner. So, we went up to deck nine and hit the Splendido buffet. Well, that is what they call it. After dinner, we went back down to the lobby bar and listened to our band for a time. Kathy called it a night early, and I stayed until the band quit, before heading back to the cabin and turning in.

Our fourth and final island stop was in the British West Indies, to the island of Grand Turk. We arrived and docked, but the weather was gloomy and overcast. I had booked a sail-and-snorkel excursion the previous evening, and Kathy and I left the boat at the same time. As soon as we disembarked, I realized that I had left my excursion ticket in my cabin. I left Kathy to go on with her shopping, and I returned to the ship to retrieve my ticket. Rushing to reach the excursion booths, I was delighted to find the booth open, but when I got in line, the guides told us the excursion had been canceled. I was left to wander about and see what I could near the port.

I again found the Harley-Davidson store and bought a T-shirt and a shot glass. I next made my way over to Jimmy Buffett's Margaritaville store and café. As it was near lunchtime, I found a table with a great view of the ocean and sat down. The decision as to what to order seemed a bit trite. What else can you do but order a margarita? I also ordered a Cheeseburger in Paradise. I know it is cliché, but I had no choice.

So here I am, sitting in the Margaritaville Café, sipping a delicious margarita, and it starts to rain. I watch the people outside scurrying to get under an umbrella or shelter. As a musician and songwriter, the inspirational muse sometimes jumps on and says, "Once around the block, and don't spare the horses." At least, that's what happened to me.

As I watched the rainfall on the most beautiful beach I had ever seen, the thought went through my head that sometimes it rains in paradise. That is when the muse kicked me, and the lyrics started pouring out. I had neither pen nor paper, but I did have my cell phone. I wanted to put this where I could find it again, so I went to the last text message Vikki ever sent me and typed the song into the reply box. The first three verses wrote themselves as I was rapidly trying to type it in one letter at a time. It took about ten minutes to get the whole thing in the phone. I would later spend a couple of hours working out the guitar chords and melody and writing the fourth and final verse.

Maybe you will run across it on Amazon or iTunes someday.

Sometimes It Rains in Paradise

Sometimes it rains in paradise,
The skies are not always blue.
I moved down here to the islands,
But it's not the same without you.

The ocean's as blue as it was in our dreams,
The islands, they never change.
The sun is warm, and the trades are cool,
But sometimes, it just rains.

I start missing you, and the skies cloud up.
The teardrops run down my face.
I pour some rum in my coffee cup,
And wipe the tears away.

The mofongo is good in Old San Juan,
The rum is good there, too.
Island music soothes my soul,
But sometimes it rains there too.

Sometimes it rains in paradise,
The skies are not always blue.
I moved down here to the islands,,
But it's not paradise without you.

Well, there it is, perhaps the best song I have ever written, as well as the easiest one. The rain stopped, and I finished my lunch. I went down to the beach and rented a mask, fins, and snorkel and got into the water. The water was nice, visibility was good, and I got some good pictures. I snorkeled for a while and then turned in the equipment and went back to the ship.

Back on board, I got a shower and changed into something comfortable. I met up with Kathy, and we settled into our evening. By the time we were out of the harbor and heading back to Miami, the wind had picked up, and the seas were running about fifteen to twenty feet. Even a ship as big as the *Splendor* will pitch and roll a bit with those seas. The line at guest services for seasickness pills and scopolamine patches was clear around the elevator and back down the far side of the lobby bar. The door to the smoking deck had been closed and locked, so we headed up to the casino so Kathy could smoke. While there, we played the penny slots. By the time I had lost fifty bucks, I was ready for something different, so we went down to the lobby bar and listened to the music.

Saturday was a sea day. No more stops until we hit Miami port on Sunday morning. We got into port about six thirty on Sunday morning, but they would not immediately let us disembark. We had to get clearance from the customs and the Port Authority. As soon as we got clearance, we heard from the overhead speakers that there was a problem in the port building that would delay our disembarkation. All morning we sat in the casino, waiting for our section to be called. Finally, about eleven o'clock, they cleared us, and we all made our way to deck three to disembark.

The escalators had stopped working early on, and the elevators were slow. That was the delaying factor. We finally got to customs and walked through with no problems. Once we were out on the sidewalk with our baggage, I left Kathy to guard the bags. I went to the parking garage to get our car. As we were docked a good mile away from the parking garage, it took me a while to get there and then get the car out of the garage.

I pulled up in front of the terminal building, and Kathy waved me to park on the other side of the street. The porter wheeled our luggage across to the car and helped Kathy and me stow it away. Some bags went into the trunk, and we put the rest in the back seat. I tipped the porter, and we were on our way home.

The drive was long and slow. Spring break was over, and all the cruise-ship traffic leaving the port clogged up the Florida Turnpike. With so many cars on the road, there were bound to be accidents—and there were. Sometimes, we came across an accident that was caused by the slowdowns, and the people involved were sitting in the median, waiting for the state patrol to arrive. About two o'clock, we got hungry, so we stopped at one of the turnpike rest areas and got some food.

Traffic finally eased up a bit, and we could proceed more swiftly. We reached Kathy's home around seven thirty that evening and unloaded her luggage. I stayed for a bit, and Kathy and I regaled her family with anecdotes from the trip. Finally, I bid Kathy good-bye and got back on the road to my house. I was home by ten thirty and unloaded the luggage from the car. I rolled into my own bed for the first time in a week, and it felt wonderful. I dropped off to sleep immediately.

The next morning, I awoke early and started the laundry. As I had cleaned house before leaving for the cruise, laundry was my only chore. I rested and took a quiet day for myself. My son had come in during the night and was sound asleep in the spare room when I got up. I just wanted to rest and get everything ready for the next big step in becoming Kimberly.

The cruise was an important step for Kimberly. For the entire week, I went about among complete strangers as a female, and was totally accepted. It is different at work where everyone knew Richard, and are now getting acquainted with Kimberly. I know for a fact that some people realized that I was a trans woman, but all accepted me. This just confirms, once again, that being Kimberly is the best of all possible directions for me to follow for the rest of my life.

Chapter Fifteen

Measure Twice, Cut Once

On Monday, March 20, 2017, I received a phone call from the surgeon's office, informing me that I needed to be at the surgery center by six thirty the next morning. Thomas and I woke early, and I got my bath. I shaved carefully and washed the surgery areas with Hibiclense, a special anti-bacterial soap for medical uses. Of course, as with any surgery, I had to be NPO, which means nothing by mouth. I couldn't even have my morning coffee.

We loaded up about 5:00 a.m. and headed for the Tallahassee and Southeastern Plastic Surgery Center. We arrive about fifteen minutes early and pressed the button positioned by the door. A few minutes went by, and someone from inside came and let us in. She walked me back to the prep area, took my vitals, and started my IV.

The anesthesiologist came in and listened to my lungs. She heard something she was not comfortable with and told the nurse to give me a breathing treatment. Thirty minutes of breathing in albuterol, and I was given a go for surgery. By then, I had an IV and a bag of fluids running. Dr. Kirbo came in and did the marking.

Since I was having two procedures at the same time, it took a bit of time to mark everything. The nurse gave me something for acid reflux, and she injected something to relax me, Valium or something like that. I really do not remember what she gave me. After a bit, she walked me into the OR, and I got on the table. The anesthesiologist started getting me prepped for twilight time. After a bit, she placed a mask over my nose and mouth and told me to breathe deeply. A few breaths later, and it was lights out for our girl Kimberly.

I have no clue what happened during the next five hours, as I was not there. If you want to know, you can look up a video of a tummy tuck and breast augmentation on YouTube at the following link: http://www.bodysculptor.com/body/mommy-makeover/ It will not be mine, but the procedure is the same, allowing for variations in technique unique to the physician.

I gradually became aware of my surroundings in PACU (the post-anesthesia care unit), and the first thing the recovery nurse did was hand me a Percocet to swallow. I did as I was asked, and then she handed me a small plastic card. I remember her telling me that the card had the serial numbers of each of the implants and not to lose it. For three weeks, that would be the last time I saw that card.

I waited a bit, and she brought in my son. She told him to get the car and bring it to the back entrance. With help, she got me into a wheelchair and rolled me out to the waiting automobile. By then, I could stand and transfer to the car without too much difficulty.

Since I had already picked up my antibiotics and pain meds, we didn't have to stop in town; we came straight to the house. Thomas helped me out of the car and into the recliner. I spent most of the rest of that day asleep. Once I got into a comfortable position, it didn't hurt much, but changing positions was seriously painful. I couldn't stand erect; I had to walk hunched over. I felt and looked like the hunchback of Notre Dame, with the emphasis on the "dame" part.

Now that I am home, I am going to backtrack a bit and discuss the details of the surgery. The breast implants were the easy part of this procedure. Dr. Kirbo first made a ten-centimeter (two-and-a-half-inch) incision along the sub mammary crease. Once he opened the incision, he made a bed in which to place the implant. He placed an implant into its bed, closed the tissue around it with dissolving sutures, and then closed the outer incision, again with dissolving sutures. He placed adhesive steri-strips over the external incisions. He made quick work of the two implants, once in place, the OR staff sat me up on the table to make sure the breasts would fall into the right place.

Now for the tummy tuck. As I was asleep at the time, I am not sure where he started. The belly button must be detached from the skin. That is the logical first step. The second step is to incise a long shallow cut through the skin from one iliac crest (hip) to the other. This is often referred to as a bikini cut. The fine, faint, almost-invisible scar will be completely hidden by a bikini bottom. The incision had a downward curve to it. The next incision is to make a similar incision from one hip to another, this time with the curve going up. Once these two incisions are made, the skin between the cuts can be removed and discarded.

Logically, the next step would be to start some liposuction. Once that is done, the upper skin is lifted and retracted out of the way. The skin is elastic enough to give the surgeon ample room for the rest of the procedure. The fascia, (the tissue covering the muscle), is then stitched and gathered up. The stitching done up and down the fascia is to effectively shorten the muscles holding in the viscera. Now, it is time for the final bit of liposuction, and then he'll be ready to close.

Before closing the last little bit of the incision, the surgeon places a Jackson-Pratt drain tube in and routes it to the left side, where it is stitched into place. The skin is pulled downward to meet up with the incision on the bottom. At this point, a new belly button is cut through the skin, and the skin is stitched to the belly button. The incision is closed using dissolving sutures, and a huge gauze pad is placed over the cut and taped into place. The breast closure is made with dissolving sutures and tape applied over them.

After the breasts were dressed, a support bra was placed on me. When the tummy tuck incision was dressed, a compression garment was placed on me as well. I was informed by the literature given me beforehand that the steri-strips on the breast incision and the tummy-tuck incisions would fall off in due time.

Once all the cuts were made and closed, I was transferred to a gurney, moved out of the surgery suite, and taken to PACU. From my experience as a rad tech in OR, I know that once the nurse anesthetist cut off the gas, I woke up just a few minutes later. Although we go to sleep all too quickly, it takes some time for the effects to wear off enough for me to awaken. At the first sign on waking, the nurse removes the endotracheal tube from the throat. Later in PACU, as I gradually became aware of my surroundings, my son was brought in. When I was awake enough, Thomas helped me get dressed. The entire procedure was done in about five hours.

The doctor requested that I come back to the office the following morning. Thomas and I set the alarm clock and got me up and dressed and into the car. At the clinic, Dr. Kirbo looked at everything and pronounced it good. He was very happy with the mobility I had and said I was healing well.

I was beyond driving, and I was in an incredible amount of pain. On television, we see these Hollywood stars having plastic surgery in the morning, and they're out shopping the next afternoon. Let me tell you here and now, in real life, it doesn't work that way. The doctor had given me a script for pain meds, and I had some pain. The first forty-eight hours were the worst.

The surgery was on a Tuesday, and by Friday, I was off the pain meds, standing erect, and moving reasonably well. Thomas stayed with me until Saturday, and then he went home. Home alone again. He left me with the kitchen mostly cleaned up and laundry done, so I was in good shape.

The next couple of weeks went by without incident. I saw the doctor once a week, and everything seemed to be healing nicely. The breast implants, for some reason, made the skin of the breast extremely sensitive to touch, almost painful. I decided that was caused by the stretching of the skin over the implants. I checked my idea with Dr. Kirbo, and he confirmed it. At the two-week mark, I thought the incision for the tummy tuck was healing well, but there was one area just to the left of my belly button that was red and looked irritated. That same area was also hard to the touch. Dr. Kirbo checked it out and ordered a round of antibiotics to see if we could make the inflammation go away. On my week-three visit, he looked at it once again, and he was unhappy. He began to believe I was growing an abscess pocket, and he didn't want it to erupt into an open wound. He decided that he needed to reopen the incision in that area and just find out what we were dealing with.

He had me get undressed and into a gown. He wanted to wait until he had seen his last patient for the day. I sat on the exam table for a couple of hours and suffered. Those things are not comfortable for any length of time. I finally had to sit up. About four thirty, he came in and had the nurse numb up the area of concern. Once I was reclined on the table, she started giving me the lidocaine.

After I waited for thirty minutes or so, the doctor came in, and they began the procedure. He reopened the incision about two inches, and although he was expecting a pus pocket, he didn't find one. The nurse removed the drain, packed the wound with gauze, and placed a gauze pad over the wound. By the time I got home, blood had soaked through the pad and into my clothes, but not badly. They also scheduled a follow-up appointment for the next week.

When I arrived for the follow-up, Dr. Kirbo decided he needed to cut some more bad, nonhealing tissue away. He had the nurse numb me up again, and he came in and cut away some more bad tissue. By the time I got home, blood had soaked through the gauze padding and through my clothes. When I undressed, the blood was still flowing. I removed the packing, repacked the wound, and placed maxi-pads over the gauze to soak up the blood. I was afraid that I was going to have to drive myself to the ER, but the bleeding finally stopped.

I went back again five days later. Once again, he cut more bad tissue out, but he said it was getting better. I asked for some pain meds this time, and he gave me a script. He also stated that he was trying to get approval from my insurance company to pay for a wound vac. I told him that I would pay if necessary. I just wanted the hole in my belly to go away and quit hurting.

I must keep reminding myself that it had only been five weeks since the surgery and that I was healing very well. Had we not hit the speed bump, I would already have gone back to work.

At my next office visit, I went to the office, and the girls came in and placed the wound vac. What with all the poking and cutting and prodding, the walls of the wound were very sore. When the wound vac was sealed into place, the nurse turned on the pump, and that thing started to draw down the wound. It hurt very much, but I knew it was going to speed up the healing process.

The wound vac. stayed on for the weekend, and on Monday, I went back to the doctor's office. He took the wound vac off and decided he needed to debride some more. The nurse numbed me up, and we were off again. He asked me to come back on Tuesday, and I did. He looked at the wound and decided to have me come back on Thursday for more debridement. The Monday debridement hurt very much. Even the lido-caine shots hurt. I wasn't sure if I could stand another debridement, but the hole just seemed to get bigger and bigger.

Thursday, Dr. Kirbo had me scheduled late in the day so he could see me after he finished his surgery cases. The nurse, a different one this time, took excellent care of me and did a thorough job of injecting the lidocaine. The numbing shots were almost painless, and even the ones that were not painless didn't hurt much. When the doctor came in and started debriding, I never felt a thing. I was very grateful to the nurse for taking her time and preparing me so well, and I told her so. Dr. Kirbo also remarked about her preparations.

When the doctor was finished, Nurse Tina repacked the wound and bandaged over the packing very thoroughly. I have had days when I would come home with blood soaking through the packing, the bandage, two maxi-pads, and my clothes. It even saturated the seat belt in the car once. This time, I experienced none of that. I was actually able to make it through the night without having to open the wound up and repack it again.

On my next visit, Adriane, his regular nurse, took me in hand. At two thirty on a Friday, there was no one at the reception desk, and I couldn't see anyone at all in the office. I was standing there waiting to let someone know I was there when I heard my name. Adriane was calling me from down the hall. She said she would come get me in a few minutes.

When Adriane walked me back, she took the wound-vac. supplies and had me sit on the exam table. I was in a maxi sundress, one I bought early on. Up until now, I hadn't been able to wear it because of the bra that was necessary to hold the prosthetics. Now, not having to use the prosthetics, I was able to wear the dress. It was nice, and it fit the new me perfectly.

I thought I would have to undress as usual and put on a paper gown, but Adriane suggested that I just pull the dress way up high, which I did, and that suited me just fine. She trimmed the foam rubber that would go in the hole and fitted it very carefully. Then she debrided just a little bit of fat from inside, and it didn't hurt. The most painful part (placing the foam) came next. Once the foam was in place, she stretched a thin, adhesive plastic sheet over the holes (there were now four, one large and three small ones, including the belly button).

With the Tegrederm in place, she made a small x-cut dead center of the major wound and attached the plastic tube. Adrian then connected the tube to the canister on the pump and started the vacuum. My goodness, that hurt when the wound started closing. The edges were very tender from being freshly cut. After the initial drawdown, the pain eased up quite a bit, and we were done for the day. I gathered up my purse, the case for the wound vac, and my tablet, and Adriane walked me up front and out of the building.

As I had not eaten at all today, I decided to go to Olive Garden and have something Italian. I overordered and ended up bringing home more than I ate. My, my, I was stuffed like a shell! My leftovers are in the fridge and will be my dinner tomorrow night, probably with a nice glass of wine. I do have some good wine chilled in the refrigerator.

Six weeks and three days have gone by since my surgery. I should have gone back to work three weeks ago. I would have, if I had not hit this speed bump. Nothing I have ever done has been easy, with one exception. Loving Vikki was the easiest thing and one of the best things in my life. Make that two exceptions. The decision to live true and become female was an easy one as well.

This is not to say that the actual transition was easy; it wasn't. But the decision to enter transition was an easy one to make. When I discovered that I could change gender and not have to live a double life or give up my career, the decision was made on the spot. I spent a great deal of time and energy researching all aspects of this decision, and the more I looked, the more right it felt. For the most part, the transition has been easy. I rushed things a bit, partly because of the biological changes but also because I was anxious to get the show on the road. I didn't want to spend one more second living a lie. I never wanted to have to wear guy clothes again. I have things that I want to do in this life, and the sooner I get started, the better and happier I will be.

I must return to Dr. Kirbo's office on Monday to make sure the wound vac is doing what it's supposed to. With luck, he will just change it out and reset it for a week. Dr. Kirbo stated on Thursday that he didn't think he would have to do any more debridement. Now that the antibiotics are taking care of any lingering infection, maybe this time I will be able to see some actual healing.

I went to Dr. Kirbo's office today and had the wound vac. removed to check the progress of the wound. Adriane got me ready, and then Dr. Kirbo came in. For the first time since the incision was reopened, Dr. Kirbo looked pleased. He said the wound looked much better and that the two smaller wounds were no longer connected to the big one. He was very happy with the progress made over the weekend and wanted me to start coming in on Mondays, Wednesdays, and Fridays to have the wound vac reset. This will also allow the doctor to monitor the progress of healing.

He ordered me another week's worth of antibiotics, and I am just beginning my second week. I think this is what is making the healing progress so rapidly after lagging for so long. We're coming up on eight weeks post-op. In maybe another month, I can go back to work. I surely hope so. Just sitting around home unable to do anything is miserable.

Two weeks have gone by, and the wound continues to heal. Last week, Dr. Kirbo changed my antibiotic and increased the amount to a twenty-day supply. He is pleased with the wound's progress and says we are over the hump. There was one little area of concern: the channel to one of the smaller openings has closed off on each end, but there is an abscess pocket trapped between. Dr. Kirbo numbed me up and opened that area so we could include it under the wound vac. When I went in yesterday, the doctor was very pleased. We restarted the wound vac, and the wound has shrunk from seven to five centimeters in diameter, which is encouraging, as it was over ten centimeters at its worst.

Dr. Kirbo wants me back on Wednesday, but since it's only to get the wound vac reset, I will only see the nurse. On Friday, he will take another look, and I think he will be happy. I know I will be. Adriane told me yesterday that I am only a couple of weeks away from being able to dispense with the wound vac and go back to work. Hip-hip hooray! I will be so glad not to be sick and to be up and out again.

I had thought there would be a revision after I finish healing, with a repeat trip to the OR and a skin graft, but Adriane told me that was not the case. Dr. Kirbo will do it on an office visit. He'll simply cut open the skin, stretch it downward to the original incision line, and reattach it, covering up the quarter-size puckered scar. I am just amazed at what they can do. I will not even have to miss a day of work. Sweet.

Three weeks have gone by, and the wound vac is history. The huge gaping hole in my belly is gone now, and all that remains is a puckered, pinkish scar. Dr. Kirbo has signed my release to go back to work full time on full duty with no restrictions, and I am very ready. I know my coworkers are as well. Bless their hearts, they have been getting slammed at work and covering my weekend shift plus all week long, so I know they are very bone-weary tired. I will have to buckle up and pull some of the load off them and let them catch up.

They have already called a couple of times wondering when I would be back and how to arrange their vacations for the summer. I have been unable to answer exactly until now. I start back on Thursday, and it will be a great relief. My checking account will surely appreciate the reversal of the negative cash flow. I was running out of money and sources for money, and I still have bills to pay including a car payment and a titty payment.

I got up this morning and showered and shaved all the spots that needed shaving. I put on my deodorant, brushed my teeth and hair, and put on my scrubs for the first time in three months. Remarkably, they still fit. I stick out in places I didn't before the surgery, and I stick in in places I didn't before losing all the belly flab, but they still fit. Wow.

I am in the car for the hour-and-a-half drive through the traffic in Tallahassee to the hospital where I work. The early-morning drives are quite nice as I watch the sun paint the sky pink, purple, and a whole rainbow of colors. The brightly colored palette reminds me how lucky I am to be living in a time when the world is changing its perception on who I am and how I can live.

That perception is changing for many people who are just now finding out about themselves in an awakening such as I have had. Although this part of my journey from male to female is over, my greatest adventure is just beginning. I have so many unanswered questions, and time alone will provide the answers.

Chapter Sixteen

Over the Rainbow

Today, I started back to work. I have healed, finally, and have picked up the return-to-work release form from Dr. Kirbo's office. I still have some swelling that will take a couple of months to go down, but, essentially, I am finally well.

When I clock in at work, I will be Kimberly. For the first time, I will look and feel very female. Okay, so I am not a bikini model. I am a sixty-three-year-old grandmother who looks really nice in my scrubs, or when I put on my fancy clothes or blue jeans and a Harley T-shirt.

To reach this point, I have undergone many changes. I did my home-work last summer after Vikki died. My transition started by recognizing that I truly needed to make a transition. I did the necessary groundwork and the research on the transgender community. Goodness, there are almost as many of us as there are left-handed people!

My official out day was September 23, 2016. I have lived as a female ever since that date. I dress appropriately, whether at work, at home, out for dinner, or shopping. I am not currently dating anyone, and I don't think that will happen soon. I am fine with that. I use the women's bathroom and never get a second look. Since the surgery made it impossible to remove my breasts, I can, most happily, dress female. No longer is it an option. I have finally put Richard aside. I haven't thought about Richard in some months now. Kimberly is fully in the driver's seat, and she has learned enough to not make too many faux pas.

I do miss Richard a bit, and I am sorry I had to let him go, but he would not have it any other way. I do hope he finds Vikki's soul. All I know is that he left here looking for her.

The transgender community is gaining strength and moving ahead with public acceptance. Just in the past year, we have added another letter to the alphabet soup. It is now LGBTQ. I meet people almost every day who know someone who is trans. I have not received any of the hostility I expected, but I know it is out there. Most people accept the fact that I am female, and if they don't, they at least keep it to themselves. My work environment is supportive, and my coworkers are getting increasingly comfortable with my new look and personality.

I will never be a makeup queen or an over-the-top drag queen. For me, it is not about the makeup or the wild, garish costumes most drag queens seem to prefer. Rather, this is about me feeling appropriately dressed for work or play or any social occasion. I will not be a recluse. I do plan to be out and about, and when I go out for the evening, I will be dressed very well. Our new first lady, Melania Trump, is the classiest dresser we have had in the White House since Jackie Kennedy. Of course, she was a professional model, and she has exquisite taste in clothes and accessories. I do hope I can mirror that to some extent. I don't have her budget, but I do very well with the clothes I buy.

I will go to the beach when I can, and when I have time and money and the weather is nice, I will be there in my tankini, soaking up rays (with properly applied sunscreen), and vitamin sea. You might see me at a movie matinee, a rock concert, or in a fine-dining establishment. Where you will not see is me hanging around with a bunch of drag queens. I simply think that if the LGBTQ community wants more acceptance, they should try harder not to be so "in your face." But maybe that is wrong as well. Everyone has the right to live as they feel they should. We all have our own opinions and most of the time should keep them to ourselves.

As transgenders, we have made great strides from such a horrid beginning. We are now guaranteed protection from discrimination in the workplace, and that translates into other public venues as well. This year marks the fact that the term "gender identity disorder" gets dropped from the mental-illness diagnosis tree. It is no longer considered a disease. "Disease" implies sickness, and "sickness" implies a need to be treated and cured. Therefore, the new term—gender dysphoria—has been added to the diagnostic tree. This describes a condition whereby the person suffering from it is acutely aware of living as the wrong gender, and this term deals with the struggle to change gender.

When this happened to the lesbian and gay parts of the community some years ago, suddenly, homosexuality became acceptable in the mainstream. No longer was it a sickness to be cured. As it turned out, there was no cure, because there was no disease. Here's hoping this acceptance happens for us transgenders as well.

Many of us tend to try to disguise who we are. This I will not do. I have been told that unless I have the vaginoplasty (have my penis, scrotum, and testes removed) and a neovagina created, I will not be a "real" woman. Well, maybe—but my thinking is that I do not need all the parts to be female. It is attitude and state of mind that makes me female. If I am asked, I will answer "female" or maybe "trans-female." If you want to know if my tits are real, I will answer. If necessary, I will show you.

There are going to be some troublesome issues going forward from here. One that I know of will come up in November, when I go to renew my driver's license. My hair will be down, my tits will be out, and I am going to do my best to get them to correct the error on my license. That damned "M" still haunts me. It's beginning to look like I might have to hire that attorney after all. I am not sure how a legal name change and an amended birth certificate will help. I am not sure I can amend the birth certificate to state that I am female. I do want to drop the Richard, but it might be better to put up with that nuisance rather than address all the issues that dropping it will create.

What began almost one year ago, in heartache and tragedy, has consumed everything I have known. Like the phoenix of mythology, I have emerged from the ashes, new and reborn and sporting the plumage of the female of the human species. In birds, the males wear the gaudy colors and dance provocatively. In humans, the females do all of this. Guess I better order that pole from Amazon.com and start working on those dance moves. If I wanted to catch a man, I would, but I don't. I will just trust that life will provide me with company and companionship. If I can't have love, then I will just give love to life, liberty, and the catching of happiness. I could have said "pursuit," but I intend to catch happiness—and a lot of it.

For once and for all, a final good-bye to my soulmate. Vikki, I will never stop loving you, and I will always be grateful that you chose me. I will always remember. Please go find Richard; he is lost and alone and out there looking for you. When you find him, give him a big hug from his second-best girl, Kimberly.

The rainbow is the symbol of our unity. All of us who do not fit the so-called norm are included within and covered by this umbrella: lesbians, gays, bisexuals, transgenders, and queers. The rainbow bridge, in Norse mythology, is the pathway from Midgard (Earth) to Asgard, home of the Gods. You must die in glorious battle as a hero before you are permitted to cross the rainbow bridge and enter Valhalla. And of course, there is always that old pot of gold waiting at the end of the rainbow legend For all of us in the LGBTQ community, the pot of gold is having our civil rights upheld and being accepted into the mainstream.

For those of us included in the rainbow, I think back to *Star Trek*, the original series. In one of the last episodes, Spock wore a strange-looking necklace with the acronym "IDIC." This represented something near and dear to my heart. The letters stand for "infinite diversity, in infinite combinations." This makes more sense when you consider the randomness of human reproduction. Human reproduction can provide infinite combinations in which DNA from two individuals comes together to form a new and unique individual. Although, as sometimes happens when dealing with statistics, a doppelganger can also fall out of the old statistical hopper. Most of the time, the genetics are random and produce uniqueness.

Many things come into play with us. Genetics, environment, upbringing, and who knows what all else figures into making a trans person. It has been observed that transgender people have been around for a long time, perhaps as long as humans have been around.

The IDIC says it all: we are a diverse species. We do not have all the answers. Every answer generates multiple questions. Nothing is cut and dry, and there is no single line of demarcation. You can't have black and white without a huge gray area. For that matter, black is the absence of color, and white is all colors mixed together. For all those racists out there: open your minds and absorb this fact! We are all human. I do not recognize any race but one: the human race. I will have to make up my mind about any we contact from other star systems when we find them; my bet is that they will be human as well. There will be differences; there always are, but those differences will have to be assimilated into the general definition of the word *human*.

Thank goodness, I survived my ride over the rainbow. I plan to enjoy my few remaining years living as a woman. It has been so much fun already, and I am looking forward to polishing Kimberly to a fine shine, like the diamond she is. There are still many unanswered questions about my future, but that is at least half the fun. I live with gusto, and I plan to make every minute count.

I learned very recently that our time is, indeed, very limited. Farewell, Richard. You will be sorely missed. I hope you find Vikki somewhere out there. I hope you find the true happiness denied you here on earth.

This is the end of the beginning, the ending of two lives and the beginning of a third. I do hope Kimberly will find other things to write about. Just maybe, down the road a bit, she will pen a sequel, but I hope she is too busy living her life. To paraphrase Spock, "May she live long and prosper."

Afterword

I wish to think all the people who had a hand in this book, as well as all of those who had an open mind and helpful heart in helping me deal with the double whammy of losing Vikki and becoming Kimberly.

Thank you, Tracy, for being there when I needed you. You were the first one I came out to. You didn't judge me. You laughed at me and with me as I took the first tentative steps into womanhood. My biggest supporter and fan, you are my BFF, now and always. You know I love you, sista.

Thank you, Pat, for sending Tracy to talk to me about the Employee Assistance Program at work. Your insight was, as always, right on the money, although for other reasons than you thought.

Thank you, Lisa, for listening to me and encouraging Kimberly to be all that she can be. Thanks for helping me put my grief in its proper niche.

Thanks to my boss and my coworkers for being understanding while the hormones were kicking my tail and for picking up the slack while I had my surgery and recovery. Sorry, guys, I really didn't think it would take this long. You all have been awesome.

Thanks to HCA. Without their forward-thinking employment policies, I would be stuck living a lie for another four years instead of being able to live true. Our hospital administration has been extremely supportive.

Thanks to my three sons. Things were a little shaky at first, but you're all on board vigorously now. My transition would not have been as successful without you all in my corner.

A very special thank you to Dr. Ben Kirbo, his head-office nurse, Adriane, and the entire staff at Southeastern Plastic Surgery Center in Tallahassee, Florida, for their dedication to their profession, their time, and their tireless efforts to get me through a very difficult recovery from major surgery. Thanks for the tits and tummy. When I look in the mirror now, thanks to you all, I see Kimberly looking back with a big smile on her face.

Thank you, Trish. As my sister-in-law, you blew me away with overwhelming support. We have known each other for twenty-five years, through marriage, divorce, and death, and you have always been there for me, as has your marvelous family. I look forward to another fun cruise someday.

Thanks to all the transgender people I have met over the last twelve months, for showing me that "different" does not mean wrong or evil.

Thank you, Dr. Waldenberger for the hug and best wishes at the Christmas party at Dr. Dellock's and Dr. Pandit's. Dr. Dellock, thank you for inviting me to the party.

Thank you, Kathy, for going on the cruise with me. We had a blast, didn't we?

Thank you, Mom and Dad. I know you didn't ever understand me, but you loved me just the same. Thank you for all that you did to bring me into this world and nurture me into adulthood.

Finally, thank you, Vikki, for loving a flawed human being with all your heart till you died. I hope I made you as happy as you did me, in the time we had.

About the Author

R. Kimberly Davis was born in the 1950s, one of the many babies born near or after the end of the Korean War. She was a member of the mini-baby boom. A high-school graduate, she ran a construction company for a few years with her brother as a partner. After marrying, she fathered three sons. She is divorced from their mother. For three years, she raised the boys alone before marrying Vikki. This began a twenty-five-year relationship that made everyone very happy and only ended in 2016 with Vikki's death. Kimberly made the decision to transition in July 2016 and officially came out of the closet September 23, 2016.

She currently resides in a small South Georgia community and is working on her second book, a science-fiction novel. She lives alone with four feline people and tries to take the best care of them that she can, even with the language barrier. The felines speak no human, and the one human speaks no Felinese.

Kimberly works as a nuclear-medicine technologist at her local hospital. She has graduated from college twice and passed two national registry exams to obtain her professional credentials, allowing her to be a licensed medical practitioner.

Kimberly says of herself, "My hair is white, and my eyes are blue. I am five feet nine inches tall, and I weigh about 195 pounds, although that is changing. Life is not about the beginning and ending dates but about the gap between. I am all over that gap and squeezing it for all the living I can get out of it."

Made in the USA
San Bernardino, CA
04 July 2017